Understanding Blockchain Beyond Cryptocurrency

By Taylor Buck

Copyright © 2024 Taylor Buck.

All rights reserved. No part of this publication may be reproduced, stored in a retrieval system, or transmitted in any form or by any means, electronic, mechanical, photocopying, recording, scanning, or otherwise, without the prior written permission of the author.
This publication is designed to provide accurate information in regards to the subject matter covered. However, the author makes no representations or warranties with respect to the accuracy or completeness of the contents of this book. It is sold with the understanding that neither the author nor the publisher is engaged in rendering legal, financial, investment, accounting, or other professional services. The author shall not be liable for any loss of profit or any other commercial damages, including but not limited to special, incidental, consequential, personal, or other damages.

First Print Edition 2024.

A Quick Note on This Book

Blockchain is a rapidly evolving technology, and while its origins are closely tied to cryptocurrencies, its potential reaches far beyond that realm. However, due to its relatively recent emergence, many people are still unaware of the broader applications of blockchain. In this book, I aim to demystify blockchain, showcasing its practical uses across various industries and highlighting how it can serve as a catalyst for creating a more collaborative, transparent, and secure future.

The information presented here is publicly available and widely accessible; nothing is proprietary or exclusive to my perspective. While this book focuses on select industries that are currently leveraging blockchain, countless others are exploring its possibilities. To fully grasp the potential of this emerging technology, continuous research is essential. By the time this book is published, there will likely be new applications and advancements in blockchain technology around the world. We live in an era of rapid technological progress, which can be overwhelming at times, but it's also what drives our curiosity and fascination with the future of innovation.

Table of Contents

Chapter 1: The Fundamentals of Blockchain Technology

Chapter 2: Blockchain in Supply Chain Management

Chapter 3: Blockchain in Healthcare

Chapter 4: Blockchain in Voting Systems

Chapter 5: Blockchain for Intellectual Property and Copyright

Chapter 6: Blockchain in Real Estate

Chapter 7: Blockchain in Finance Beyond Cryptocurrencies

Chapter 8: Blockchain for Energy Markets

Chapter 9: Blockchain in Education

Chapter 10: Emerging Trends and Challenges for Blockchain

Chapter 11: The Future of Blockchain Beyond Cryptocurrency

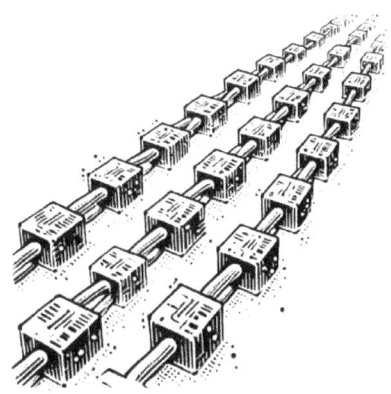

Chapter 1

The Fundamentals of Blockchain Technology

Blockchain technology is more than a buzzword; it is a revolution in how data is stored, verified, and transferred. Initially, it gained fame as the backbone of Bitcoin, but its potential reaches far beyond cryptocurrencies. At its core, blockchain is a distributed digital ledger that records transactions across multiple computers in such a way that the registered transactions are immutable (indisputable) and transparent.

For anyone trying to grasp blockchain, it's crucial to understand that it's a **trustless system**—meaning *it doesn't require a central authority like a bank or government to validate transactions*. Instead, the verification process happens through consensus, and it's cryptographically secure. Still confused? That's okay. In this chapter, we'll delve deep into what blockchain is, how it works, and its potential to transform industries outside of cryptocurrency.

What is Blockchain Technology?

At its most basic level, blockchain is a type of database. But unlike traditional databases controlled by a central authority, blockchain is **decentralized**. This means that control over the database is distributed among multiple nodes (computers), each with equal authority. The decentralization of control is one of the core principles that make blockchain technology revolutionary.

A blockchain database is structured quite differently from the typical relational databases (such as SQL databases) most people are familiar with. Traditional databases organize data into rows, columns, and tables, which makes it efficient for searching and editing large sets of data. Blockchain, on the other hand, organizes data into blocks.

Each block contains a set of transactions, and these blocks are linked together to form a chain—hence the name blockchain. Once a block is added to the chain, it is immutable, meaning it cannot be altered without altering every subsequent block, which would require control of the majority of the network (an improbable feat). This immutability ensures the security and reliability of blockchain records.

How Blockchain Works: The Building Blocks

To fully appreciate the scope of blockchain technology, we need to understand its building blocks:

Blocks

A block is a batch of data (usually transactions) that is verified by the blockchain network. Each block includes:

- A block header that contains metadata, such as a timestamp and a reference to the previous block.
- A block body that contains a list of transactions.

The block header includes a cryptographic hash (message) of the previous block, linking them together in chronological order and creating a chain.

Nodes

Nodes are individual computers or devices on the blockchain network. They store copies of the entire blockchain and help validate transactions. There are two types of nodes:

- Full nodes, which store the entire blockchain and participate in the verification process.
- Light nodes, which store only parts of the blockchain and rely on full nodes for transaction verification.

Consensus Mechanisms

Since blockchain is decentralized, no single entity can control the network. To validate transactions and maintain the integrity of the blockchain, the network must agree on the state of the blockchain. This agreement is achieved through a consensus mechanism. The most common ones are:

- Proof of Work (PoW): Used by Bitcoin, this requires network participants (miners) to solve complex cryptographic puzzles to validate transactions and add them to the blockchain. While secure, PoW is energy-intensive and slow.
- Proof of Stake (PoS): PoS replaces the energy-intensive process with a mechanism where participants validate transactions based on the number of tokens they hold. It's faster and more environmentally friendly than PoW.
- Delegated Proof of Stake (DPoS): This is a variation of PoS where token holders vote to elect delegates who validate transactions on their behalf.

Decentralization

The decentralization of blockchain is one of its most important and defining characteristics. Unlike centralized systems controlled by a single entity, blockchain distributes control among all participants. This eliminates single points of failure and makes the system more secure and transparent.

A simple example of decentralization in blockchain can be seen in file storage. In traditional systems, files are stored on centralized servers owned by companies like Google or Dropbox. With blockchain-based decentralized storage (like Filecoin), files are broken up and distributed across multiple computers (nodes) on the network. This means no single company controls your data, making it more secure, harder to hack, and giving users more control over their own information.

The Role of Cryptography in Blockchain

At the heart of blockchain's security is cryptography. Cryptography ensures the privacy and integrity of transactions on the blockchain. There are two key cryptographic concepts used in blockchain:

Hashing

A cryptographic hash function takes an input (or "message") and returns a fixed-length string of characters, which appears random. This output is known as the hash value or simply hash. For example, Bitcoin uses the SHA-256 hashing algorithm. Hash functions have two key properties:

- Deterministic: The same input will always produce the same output.
- Irreversible: It is computationally infeasible to reverse the process and find the original input given only the output.

Hashes are crucial in linking blocks together in the blockchain. Each block contains a hash of the previous block, creating an immutable chain. If anyone tries to tamper with a block, the hash changes, making the alteration immediately obvious.

Digital Signatures

Blockchain also relies on public key cryptography to ensure that transactions are authentic. Each participant has a public key and a private key. When they initiate a transaction, they sign it with their private key, creating a unique digital signature. Other participants can use the sender's public key to verify that the signature matches the transaction. This ensures that transactions are legitimate and originated from the correct source.

Smart Contracts: The Future of Automation

One of the most exciting innovations that blockchain enables is smart contracts. Smart contracts are self-executing contracts where the terms of the agreement are written into code. They automatically execute actions when predetermined conditions are met.

For example, imagine a smart contract in a real estate transaction. Instead of relying on intermediaries (lawyers, banks), the contract could be programmed to release the property title to the buyer and the payment to the seller once both parties meet the contract's conditions. This reduces costs, speeds up transactions, and eliminates the potential for fraud.

Smart contracts are most commonly associated with the Ethereum blockchain, which was designed specifically to support them. However, many blockchains now support smart contracts, as they open up endless possibilities for automation and efficiency in various industries.

Permissioned vs. Permissionless Blockchains

Not all blockchains are created equal. There are two main types of blockchains:

Permissionless Blockchains

In a permissionless blockchain (like Bitcoin or Ethereum), anyone can join the network, validate transactions, and add blocks to the chain. These blockchains are fully decentralized and open to the public. They are also more secure and censorship-resistant because of their openness. However, they tend to be slower and require more computational resources.

Permissioned Blockchains

Permissioned blockchains restrict who can participate in the network. These are often used by enterprises and governments that need control over who can access and validate transactions. While permissioned blockchains sacrifice some decentralization, they offer greater efficiency and scalability, which makes them suitable for industries like finance, healthcare, and supply chain management.

Blockchain's Strengths and Weaknesses

Blockchain technology has a wide range of strengths, but it also faces several challenges.

Strengths:

Security

Blockchain's decentralization and cryptographic security make it resistant to hacking and tampering. Once data is recorded on the blockchain, it is virtually impossible to alter it without controlling a majority of the network.

Transparency

All participants on a blockchain network can view the history of transactions, making the system highly transparent. This is particularly useful for industries like supply chain management, where transparency is critical.

Immutability

The immutability of blockchain data is one of its key strengths. Once a block is added to the chain, it cannot be altered. This makes blockchain an ideal solution for record-keeping and verification purposes.

Decentralization

Blockchain's decentralized nature removes the need for intermediaries like banks, lawyers, or brokers. This reduces costs, speeds up processes, and eliminates single points of failure.

Weaknesses:

Scalability

One of blockchain's biggest challenges is scalability. Public blockchains like Bitcoin and Ethereum struggle to handle large volumes of transactions due to their consensus mechanisms. Solutions like layer-2 scaling (such as the Lightning Network for Bitcoin) and sharding (breaking the blockchain into smaller pieces) are being developed to address this issue.

Energy Consumption

Proof of Work blockchains (like Bitcoin) consume massive amounts of energy because of the computational power required to solve cryptographic puzzles. This has raised environmental concerns. Proof of Stake and other consensus mechanisms aim to reduce energy consumption.

Regulatory Uncertainty

Blockchain exists in a legal grey area in many parts of the world. Governments are still figuring out how to regulate blockchain technology, which creates uncertainty for businesses looking to adopt it.

Complexity

Blockchain can be difficult for the average person to understand and use. While blockchain-based applications are becoming more user-friendly, there is still a significant learning curve that could hinder widespread adoption.

Summary Thoughts

Blockchain technology is more than just the foundation of cryptocurrencies like Bitcoin. *It represents a fundamental shift in how we store, verify, and transfer data.* By understanding its building blocks—blocks, nodes, consensus mechanisms, cryptography, and smart contracts—we can begin to see its potential to disrupt industries ranging from finance to healthcare.

In the following chapters, we'll explore specific use cases of blockchain beyond cryptocurrency, shedding light on its real-world applications and the challenges that remain for its broader adoption.

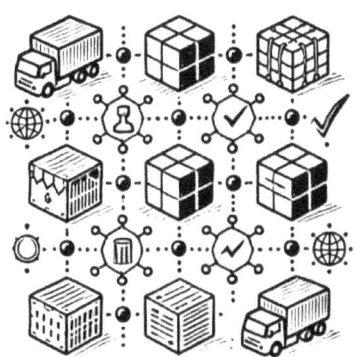

Chapter 2

Blockchain in Supply Chain Management

The supply chain is the backbone of the global economy. It encompasses everything from the sourcing of raw materials to the delivery of finished products to consumers. Modern supply chains are incredibly complex, often spanning multiple countries and involving a vast network of suppliers, manufacturers, distributors, and retailers. Managing and tracking these vast networks has traditionally been a challenge for businesses.

Issues like lack of transparency, inefficiency, fraud, and delayed communication plague global supply chains, leading to billions of dollars in losses every year. Blockchain technology is emerging as a solution to many of these problems by providing an immutable, transparent, and decentralized ledger for recording and tracking the movement of goods and services. In this chapter, we'll examine how blockchain is revolutionizing supply chain management and dive into real-world examples where it is already being implemented.

The Current State of Supply Chain Management

To understand how blockchain can improve supply chain management, it's crucial to first understand the traditional problems that companies face.

Lack of Transparency

Supply chains often involve multiple layers of suppliers and intermediaries, making it difficult for companies to gain visibility into every stage of the process. For example, a food company may source ingredients from dozens of farms and processors before the final product reaches consumers. If one supplier doesn't disclose important information—such as the use of harmful chemicals or unethical labor practices—it can taint the entire supply chain.

Inefficiency

Paper-based record-keeping is still common in many industries. These manual systems are prone to errors, delays, and miscommunication. If documents get lost, shipments may be delayed, which can lead to stockouts, customer dissatisfaction, or even perishable goods going to waste.

Fraud and Counterfeiting

Fraud is a significant issue in supply chains, particularly in industries like luxury goods, pharmaceuticals, and food. Counterfeit products enter the market, costing businesses billions in lost revenue and damaging consumer trust. In the pharmaceutical industry alone, counterfeit drugs pose serious health risks, making traceability a crucial concern.

Fragmented Data Systems

In many supply chains, each participant uses its own internal data system to manage inventory, shipments, and contracts. These systems often do not communicate well with each other, leading to data silos. This fragmentation makes it difficult to get a real-time view of the entire supply chain and often results in delays and increased costs.

How Blockchain Solves These Problems

Blockchain technology provides an ideal solution to many of the supply chain challenges outlined above. By offering an immutable and transparent ledger, blockchain can revolutionize how businesses track goods, ensure authenticity, and communicate across the supply chain.

Improved Transparency and Traceability

One of the most significant benefits of blockchain in the supply chain is its ability to provide end-to-end transparency. Every transaction on a blockchain is recorded and time-stamped, creating a digital audit trail that can be accessed by all participants in the supply chain.

For example, in the food industry, companies like Walmart are using blockchain to track the journey of food products from farm to table. Using IBM's Food Trust blockchain platform, Walmart can trace the origin of mangoes in just 2.2 seconds, compared to the six days it used to take with traditional methods. This level of traceability allows companies to respond quickly to food safety issues like contamination or recalls, minimizing the impact on consumers and protecting brand reputation.

Reducing Inefficiencies

By replacing manual, paper-based systems with a digital ledger, blockchain can greatly improve efficiency in supply chain management. Smart contracts—self-executing contracts coded into the blockchain—automatically trigger actions when certain conditions are met, such as releasing payment when a shipment is delivered.

For example, the logistics industry can benefit from blockchain by automating the process of verifying shipments. Traditionally, shipping documents like bills of lading are manually signed and verified at each stage of the supply chain. With blockchain, these documents can be stored digitally and accessed by all relevant parties. The shipment's progress can be tracked in real time, and once it reaches its destination, smart contracts can automatically trigger the payment process.

Preventing Fraud and Counterfeiting

Blockchain's immutable nature makes it an effective tool for combating fraud and counterfeiting. Each time a product changes hands in the supply chain, the transaction is recorded on the blockchain, and the product's provenance can be traced back to its origin.

In the pharmaceutical industry, blockchain can help prevent the distribution of counterfeit drugs. By tracking the movement of drugs from the manufacturer to the pharmacy, blockchain ensures that every step in the supply chain is transparent and verified. Companies like MediLedger are working with pharmaceutical giants to implement blockchain-based solutions that verify the authenticity of drugs and prevent counterfeiting.

Streamlining Communication and Collaboration

Blockchain's decentralized nature ensures that all participants in a supply chain have access to the same real-time data. This eliminates the need for multiple, disconnected data systems and streamlines communication across the supply chain.

For example, a manufacturer, supplier, and retailer can all access the same blockchain ledger to track the status of a shipment. If there's a delay or a problem with a shipment, all parties are immediately informed, reducing miscommunication and speeding up the resolution of issues. This real-time collaboration can significantly improve the efficiency and reliability of supply chains.

Case Study: Walmart and IBM Food Trust

Walmart, one of the world's largest retailers, has been at the forefront of using blockchain technology to improve supply chain transparency. In partnership with IBM, Walmart launched the **Food Trust** blockchain platform, which enables the company to trace the origin of its food products quickly and accurately.

The Problem

Walmart sources food products from thousands of suppliers worldwide. Ensuring the quality and safety of these products is a top priority, but the complexity of the supply chain makes it difficult to track the origin of food items quickly. In the event of a foodborne illness outbreak or contamination, it could take days or even weeks to identify the source of the problem, during which time more consumers could be affected.

The Solution

By using blockchain, Walmart can trace the journey of food products from farm to shelf in real time. When a product is added to the blockchain, each step of its journey—harvesting, processing, packaging, and distribution—is recorded and time-stamped. If there's an issue, Walmart can pinpoint the exact source of contamination and take immediate action to remove affected products from the shelves.

The Impact

The ability to trace food products in seconds rather than days has had a significant impact on food safety and supply chain efficiency. In a pilot program, Walmart used the Food Trust blockchain to trace the origin of mangoes from farms in Mexico to store shelves in the U.S. What used to take six days now takes just 2.2 seconds, allowing Walmart to respond quickly to potential safety issues.

Walmart is now expanding its use of blockchain to include more products and suppliers, and other retailers are following suit.

Case Study: Maersk's TradeLens Platform

The global shipping industry is another area where blockchain is making waves. **Maersk**, the world's largest container shipping company, has partnered with IBM to launch **TradeLens**, a blockchain-based platform that aims to digitize and streamline global shipping.

The Problem

The shipping industry is notoriously inefficient, with paper-based documentation, customs clearances, and manual processes causing delays and increasing costs. In many cases, a single shipment may require up to 200 separate interactions between different parties, including shippers, customs authorities, port operators, and freight forwarders. These processes are often fragmented and prone to miscommunication, resulting in costly delays.

The Solution

TradeLens provides a digital platform where all participants in the shipping supply chain can access real-time information about shipments. Using blockchain, TradeLens ensures that every transaction—whether it's a customs clearance, a container handoff, or a shipping manifest—is recorded in a shared, immutable ledger.

The Impact

TradeLens has already been adopted by over 90 organizations, including shipping companies, port operators, and customs authorities. By digitizing the shipping process and providing real-time visibility, TradeLens has reduced paperwork, streamlined customs clearances, and improved the efficiency of global trade. In one case, the platform helped reduce the time it takes to transport goods from Europe to the United States by 40%.

Blockchain's Role in Ethical Supply Chains

Beyond efficiency and fraud prevention, blockchain is also playing a critical role in creating more ethical supply chains. In industries like fashion, mining, and agriculture, consumers and regulators are increasingly demanding transparency about the social and environmental impact of products. Blockchain provides a way for companies to prove that their products are ethically sourced and produced.

Fashion Industry

In the fashion industry, blockchain can be used to track the journey of clothing from the cotton farm to the retail store. Brands like **Provenance** are using blockchain to verify the sustainability and ethical sourcing of materials used in clothing. By scanning a QR code on a product, consumers can access detailed information about the product's origin and the conditions under which it was made.

Mining Industry

In the mining industry, blockchain is being used to track the journey of minerals like cobalt, which is used in batteries for electric vehicles. Companies like **Circulor** are using blockchain to ensure that the cobalt used in their products is ethically sourced and free from child labor. This level of transparency helps companies meet regulatory requirements and build trust with consumers.

Challenges to Blockchain Adoption in Supply Chains

While the benefits of blockchain in supply chains are clear, there are still several challenges to its widespread adoption:

Integration with Existing Systems

Many companies already have established supply chain management systems in place. Integrating blockchain with these legacy systems can be complex and costly. Additionally, supply chain participants may be reluctant to share sensitive data on a shared platform, even if it is secure and transparent.

Scalability

Blockchain's scalability is a significant concern for industries that process large volumes of transactions. Public blockchains, like Bitcoin and Ethereum, have limited throughput, which could lead to delays in processing transactions. While permissioned blockchains offer better scalability, they sacrifice some of the decentralization that makes blockchain so appealing.

Regulatory Uncertainty

In many parts of the world, there is still uncertainty about how blockchain technology will be regulated. Governments are grappling with questions about data privacy, security, and liability. This regulatory uncertainty can slow down blockchain adoption, as companies are hesitant to invest in a technology that may face future legal hurdles.

Standardization

For blockchain to be fully effective in supply chains, there needs to be standardization across industries and regions. Currently, there are multiple blockchain platforms, each with its own protocols and standards. Without a unified standard, it can be difficult for companies to collaborate effectively across the supply chain.

Summary Thoughts

Blockchain technology has the potential to transform supply chain management by providing greater transparency, reducing inefficiencies, preventing fraud, and improving communication. As we've seen from real-world examples like Walmart's Food Trust and Maersk's TradeLens, blockchain is already making a tangible impact in industries ranging from food to shipping.

However, challenges like scalability, integration with existing systems, and regulatory uncertainty remain. As these challenges are addressed and blockchain continues to evolve, its role in supply chains will only grow.

Chapter 3

Blockchain in Healthcare

The healthcare sector faces numerous challenges that hinder efficiency, patient care, and overall effectiveness. Data fragmentation, lack of interoperability, privacy concerns, and escalating costs are just a few of the systemic issues plaguing the industry. The rise of digital health technologies, including electronic health records (EHRs), telemedicine, and wearable devices, has only amplified these problems, leading to an urgent need for innovative solutions that can streamline processes and enhance patient care.

Blockchain technology has emerged as a powerful tool capable of addressing many of these challenges. By providing a secure, decentralized, and transparent platform for managing medical data, blockchain can facilitate interoperability, enhance patient privacy, reduce administrative burdens, and improve data integrity. This chapter will explore how blockchain technology is revolutionizing healthcare, focusing on its applications, benefits, challenges, and future potential.

The Current Landscape of Healthcare Data Management

Data Fragmentation and Accessibility Issues

Healthcare data is often stored across various systems, including hospitals, private practices, laboratories, and insurance companies. This fragmentation leads to challenges in accessing a comprehensive view of a patient's medical history. Healthcare providers may struggle to obtain essential information when treating patients, which can result in delays, unnecessary tests, and even medical errors.

For example, a patient visiting a new healthcare provider may find that their previous medical records are unavailable, requiring them to undergo redundant tests. This not only frustrates patients but also adds to the overall costs of healthcare.

Lack of Interoperability

The lack of interoperability between different EHR systems is another critical challenge. Each healthcare organization may use different software and data formats, making it difficult to share information across platforms. Without a standardized approach to data sharing, healthcare providers may miss crucial information that could inform treatment decisions.

Interoperability issues can also impede research and population health initiatives. Researchers often struggle to access diverse datasets needed to conduct meaningful analyses, slowing the pace of medical advancements.

Security and Privacy Concerns

The sensitive nature of healthcare data makes it a prime target for cybercriminals. Data breaches in healthcare organizations can lead to severe consequences, including identity theft and fraud. According to a report by IBM, healthcare data breaches cost the industry an average of $6.5 million per incident.

Moreover, patients often have little control over who accesses their medical records. Existing systems may not provide sufficient protection for patient privacy, leaving individuals vulnerable to unauthorized access and misuse of their information.

Administrative Burdens and Costs

The administrative complexities in healthcare contribute to rising costs. Healthcare providers spend significant time and resources on billing, insurance claims processing, and compliance with regulations. In fact, administrative costs account for nearly 25% of total healthcare expenditures in the United States.

This inefficiency not only strains healthcare organizations but also detracts from the quality of care that patients receive. Providers may find themselves overwhelmed with paperwork instead of focusing on patient interactions and treatment.

Blockchain: A Transformative Solution for Healthcare

Blockchain technology, originally developed for cryptocurrencies like Bitcoin, offers a promising solution to the challenges facing the healthcare industry. By providing a decentralized, secure, and transparent platform for managing data, blockchain can address issues related to data fragmentation, interoperability, security, and administrative burdens.

Decentralization and Security

At its core, blockchain is a decentralized ledger that records transactions across a network of computers. This decentralization enhances security by eliminating single points of failure and making it significantly harder for hackers to compromise the system. Each transaction is encrypted and linked to previous transactions, creating an immutable record that is resistant to tampering.

In healthcare, this means that patient data can be stored securely on the blockchain, ensuring that only authorized individuals have access. By giving patients control over their medical records, blockchain enhances privacy while providing a reliable method for verifying the authenticity of information.

Interoperability Through Shared Standards

Blockchain can facilitate interoperability among different healthcare systems by providing a shared platform for data exchange. With blockchain, healthcare organizations can access a unified, tamper-proof record of patient information, regardless of the specific EHR system they use. This promotes seamless data sharing and collaboration among providers.

Smart contracts—self-executing contracts with the terms of the agreement directly written into code—can further enhance interoperability. For example, a smart contract could automate the sharing of specific patient data between providers, ensuring that critical information is available at the point of care.

Enhanced Patient Control and Consent Management

Blockchain technology empowers patients by giving them greater control over their medical records. Patients can grant access to their data selectively, allowing healthcare providers to view specific information as needed. This patient-centered approach not only enhances privacy but also fosters trust between patients and providers.

Smart contracts can also streamline consent management, ensuring that patients are informed about how their data will be used and shared. For instance, a patient could provide consent for a specific research study via a smart contract, which would automatically grant researchers access to relevant data while maintaining privacy protections.

Improved Data Integrity and Auditability

Blockchain's immutable nature ensures that once data is entered into the system, it cannot be altered or deleted. This feature is particularly valuable in healthcare, where data integrity is critical for making informed treatment decisions. With blockchain, healthcare providers can trust that the information they are accessing is accurate and up-to-date.

Additionally, blockchain enables easy auditability of transactions. Organizations can track who accessed patient records, what changes were made, and when these actions occurred. This transparency can help mitigate concerns about data misuse and enhance accountability in healthcare.

Applications of Blockchain in Healthcare

Secure Medical Records Management

One of the most promising applications of blockchain in healthcare is the secure management of electronic health records (EHRs). By leveraging blockchain, healthcare organizations can create a decentralized system for storing and sharing patient data.

For example, **Medicalchain** is a blockchain-based platform that allows patients to store their medical records securely and share them with healthcare providers as needed. This system enhances patient control while facilitating data exchange between providers, improving the overall quality of care.

Drug Supply Chain Management

Counterfeit drugs pose a significant threat to patient safety and public health. Blockchain can enhance the transparency and traceability of the pharmaceutical supply chain, ensuring that drugs are sourced, manufactured, and distributed safely.

MediLedger is a blockchain solution focused on improving drug supply chain integrity. By using blockchain, MediLedger enables pharmaceutical companies to verify the authenticity of drugs at every stage of the supply chain, reducing the risk of counterfeit products entering the market.

Clinical Trials and Research

Blockchain technology can improve the efficiency and integrity of clinical trials by providing a secure platform for managing trial data. By recording all trial data on the blockchain, researchers can ensure that results are tamper-proof and transparent.

PharmaLedger is an initiative that aims to enhance collaboration in clinical trials through blockchain technology. By providing a secure and transparent platform for managing trial data, PharmaLedger can improve accountability and streamline the research process.

Telemedicine and Remote Patient Monitoring

As telemedicine and remote patient monitoring gain popularity, blockchain can play a crucial role in securing patient data and ensuring privacy. By leveraging blockchain technology, healthcare providers can securely share patient data collected from remote monitoring devices, enhancing the quality of care.

Guardtime is a blockchain-based solution focused on securing telemedicine interactions and remote patient monitoring data. By using blockchain, Guardtime ensures that patient data remains private and accessible only to authorized providers.

Benefits of Blockchain in Healthcare

Enhanced Security and Privacy

Blockchain technology provides a secure and tamper-proof system for managing sensitive healthcare data. By encrypting patient information and limiting access to authorized individuals, blockchain enhances data privacy and protects against cyber threats.

Improved Data Sharing and Interoperability

Blockchain facilitates seamless data sharing among healthcare providers, enabling them to access a comprehensive view of a patient's medical history. This interoperability improves care coordination and reduces the risk of medical errors.

Increased Patient Control and Trust

By giving patients control over their medical records and allowing them to grant access selectively, blockchain fosters trust and engagement in healthcare. Patients are more likely to share their information when they know who can access it and how it will be used.

Reduced Administrative Costs

The automation of processes through smart contracts can significantly reduce administrative burdens in healthcare. By streamlining billing, claims processing, and documentation, blockchain can help healthcare organizations lower costs and allocate resources more effectively.

Challenges to Blockchain Adoption in Healthcare

Despite its potential, several challenges must be addressed before blockchain can achieve widespread adoption in healthcare.

Regulatory Hurdles

The healthcare industry is heavily regulated, and compliance with existing laws (such as HIPAA in the U.S.) can pose challenges for blockchain implementation. Organizations must ensure that their blockchain solutions meet regulatory requirements related to data privacy and security.

Integration with Legacy Systems

Many healthcare organizations use legacy systems for their operations, making it difficult to integrate blockchain technology seamlessly. Organizations may face significant costs and challenges in transitioning to blockchain-based solutions.

Data Standardization

For blockchain to be effective in healthcare, there needs to be standardization in how medical data is recorded and shared. Currently, different healthcare organizations use various data formats, which can hinder the implementation of a unified blockchain system.

Scalability Issues

Blockchain scalability remains a concern, particularly for public blockchains that may struggle to handle the high transaction volumes associated with healthcare. Solutions like layer-2 scaling and private blockchains may be necessary to address these scalability challenges.

Case Studies in Blockchain Healthcare Implementation

Estonia's E-Health System

Estonia is one of the leading countries in adopting blockchain technology for healthcare. The Estonian eHealth system uses blockchain to secure patient data and ensure its integrity. Patients have control over their medical records and can grant access to healthcare providers as needed.

The system also tracks who accesses patient records, ensuring accountability and transparency. By leveraging blockchain, Estonia has created a more efficient and secure healthcare system that empowers patients and improves collaboration among healthcare providers.

IBM Watson Health

IBM Watson Health is utilizing blockchain technology to enhance data sharing among healthcare providers. By creating a secure platform for managing medical records, IBM aims to improve patient care and reduce administrative burdens.

Watson Health also leverages AI and data analytics to provide actionable insights to healthcare providers, enabling them to make informed decisions based on comprehensive patient data.

Summary Thoughts

Blockchain technology holds immense potential to revolutionize healthcare by addressing long-standing issues related to data fragmentation, security, and inefficiency. By providing a secure, decentralized platform for managing medical records, drug supply chains, clinical trials, and billing processes, blockchain can enhance patient care and reduce costs across the healthcare system.

However, significant challenges must be overcome to realize this potential, including regulatory hurdles, integration with existing systems, scalability concerns, and the need for data standardization. As healthcare organizations continue to explore blockchain solutions, it is essential to address these challenges proactively.

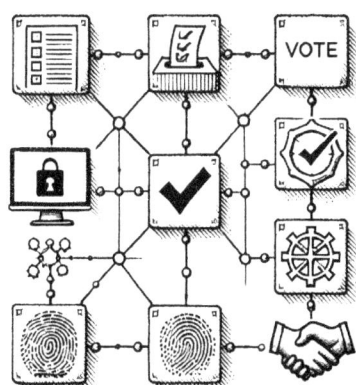

Chapter 4

Blockchain in Voting Systems

Voting is a cornerstone of democracy, enabling citizens to express their preferences and elect representatives. However, the integrity of voting systems has come under scrutiny in recent years, with concerns about voter fraud, cyber threats, and the transparency of election processes. Traditional voting methods often face challenges related to security, accessibility, and trust, leading to calls for innovative solutions that can enhance the electoral process.

Blockchain technology has emerged as a promising tool for revolutionizing voting systems. By providing a secure, transparent, and tamper-proof platform for casting and counting votes, blockchain can enhance the integrity of elections, increase voter participation, and restore public trust in democratic processes. In this chapter, we will explore how blockchain technology is transforming voting systems, focusing on its applications, benefits, challenges, and future potential.

The Current Landscape of Voting Systems

Vulnerabilities in Traditional Voting Methods

Traditional voting methods, whether paper ballots or electronic voting machines, often face various vulnerabilities that can undermine the electoral process. Some common issues include:

- **Voter Fraud:** Concerns about voter impersonation, ballot stuffing, and other forms of fraud can erode public confidence in elections. While instances of widespread fraud are rare, even the perception of vulnerability can impact voter turnout and trust in the system.

- **Cybersecurity Threats:** As elections increasingly rely on technology, the risk of cyberattacks on voting systems has grown. High-profile incidents, such as the 2016 U.S. presidential election, highlighted the potential for foreign interference and hacking attempts aimed at manipulating election outcomes.

- **Lack of Transparency:** Many traditional voting systems operate as "black boxes," making it difficult for voters to verify that their votes were counted accurately. This lack of transparency can lead to doubts about the legitimacy of election results.

- **Accessibility Challenges:** Traditional voting methods may not be accessible to all citizens, particularly those with disabilities or those living in remote areas. Ensuring that everyone can participate in elections is essential for a healthy democracy.

The Importance of Trust in the Electoral Process

Trust is a fundamental component of democratic elections. When citizens believe that the electoral process is fair, transparent, and secure, they are more likely to participate. Conversely, doubts about the integrity of elections can lead to apathy and disengagement.

Building and maintaining trust in the electoral process requires robust safeguards, transparent procedures, and reliable technologies. Blockchain has the potential to address these concerns by providing a secure and auditable platform for voting.

How Blockchain Can Enhance Voting Systems

Blockchain technology offers several advantages that can address the vulnerabilities of traditional voting methods. Some key applications include:

- **Secure Voter Registration:** Blockchain can streamline the voter registration process by creating a secure and tamper-proof record of registered voters. This system can help prevent voter fraud and ensure that only eligible individuals can participate in elections.

- **Casting Votes:** With blockchain, voters can cast their ballots securely from any device with internet access. By using cryptographic signatures, each vote can be verified while maintaining voter anonymity.

- **Counting Votes:** Blockchain allows for real-time counting of votes, ensuring that results are available quickly and accurately. The decentralized nature of blockchain also means that results can be independently verified by multiple parties, increasing transparency.

- **Auditability:** The immutable nature of blockchain makes it easy to audit election results. Voter records can be traced and verified, allowing independent observers to confirm the accuracy of the election outcome.

Case Study: Estonian E-Voting System

Estonia is often cited as a pioneer in adopting blockchain technology for voting. The country implemented an e-voting system in 2005, allowing citizens to cast their votes online securely. The system leverages blockchain technology to enhance security and transparency.

In Estonia's e-voting system, each vote is recorded on a blockchain, providing an immutable record that can be independently verified. Voters can use their national ID cards to authenticate their identities and cast their votes remotely. The system has been praised for its efficiency and has been successfully used in multiple elections.

Voatz: A Mobile Voting Platform

Voatz is a mobile voting platform that uses blockchain technology to enable secure voting for citizens, particularly those living abroad or with disabilities. The platform allows voters to cast their ballots using their smartphones while ensuring the integrity and anonymity of their votes.

Voatz employs biometric authentication and cryptographic techniques to secure votes. Each vote is recorded on a blockchain, providing a transparent and auditable record of the election. The platform has been used in various local elections in the United States and has received positive feedback for its accessibility and security features.

Horizon State: A Blockchain Voting Platform

Horizon State is a blockchain-based voting platform that enables organizations and communities to conduct secure and transparent elections. The platform provides a decentralized infrastructure for managing the entire voting process, from registration to vote counting.

Horizon State uses blockchain technology to ensure the integrity of votes and enhance transparency. The platform allows voters to cast their ballots using a secure app, and all votes are recorded on a blockchain, providing an immutable record that can be audited.

Benefits of Blockchain in Voting Systems

Enhanced Security and Integrity

Blockchain technology enhances the security and integrity of the voting process. By creating a decentralized and tamper-proof record of votes, blockchain reduces the risk of voter fraud and manipulation.

Increased Transparency and Trust

The transparent nature of blockchain allows voters to verify that their votes were counted accurately. This transparency fosters trust in the electoral process, encouraging greater participation among citizens.

Improved Accessibility

Blockchain voting systems can enhance accessibility for voters, particularly those with disabilities or those living in remote areas. By enabling secure remote voting, blockchain can ensure that all citizens have the opportunity to participate in elections.

Faster Results and Audits

With blockchain technology, election results can be counted in real-time, providing quicker access to outcomes. Additionally, the immutable nature of blockchain allows for easy auditing of election results, ensuring accountability and integrity.

Challenges to Blockchain Adoption in Voting Systems

Despite its potential, several challenges must be addressed to achieve widespread adoption of blockchain in voting systems.

Regulatory and Legal Hurdles

The legal and regulatory landscape for voting is complex and varies by jurisdiction. Ensuring that blockchain voting systems comply with existing laws and regulations can be a significant challenge. Policymakers must establish clear guidelines for the use of blockchain in elections.

Technological Barriers

Implementing blockchain technology in voting systems requires significant investment in infrastructure, training, and cybersecurity measures. Organizations must ensure that their systems are secure and reliable before deploying blockchain-based voting solutions.

Public Perception and Trust

While blockchain has the potential to enhance trust in the electoral process, public perception of technology can be a barrier. Educating voters about blockchain technology and addressing concerns about its security and reliability is essential for successful adoption.

Digital Divide and Accessibility Issues

While blockchain can enhance accessibility for many voters, there remains a digital divide that must be addressed. Ensuring that all citizens have access to the necessary technology and internet connectivity is crucial for the success of blockchain voting systems.

Future Directions for Blockchain in Voting Systems

Increased Adoption of Hybrid Models

As more jurisdictions explore blockchain technology for voting, we may see the emergence of hybrid models that combine traditional voting methods with blockchain-based solutions. This approach can leverage the strengths of both systems while addressing the challenges of adoption.

Collaborative Efforts Among Stakeholders

Successful implementation of blockchain voting systems will require collaboration among various stakeholders, including government agencies, technology providers, and civil society organizations. By working together, stakeholders can develop secure and reliable voting solutions that meet the needs of voters.

Research and Development

Ongoing research and development in blockchain technology will be critical to overcoming existing challenges. Innovations in scalability, security, and interoperability can enhance the effectiveness of blockchain in voting systems.

Summary Thoughts

Blockchain technology has the potential to revolutionize voting systems by enhancing security, transparency, and accessibility. By providing a decentralized and tamper-proof platform for casting and counting votes, blockchain can restore public trust in democratic processes and encourage greater participation.

While challenges remain, including regulatory hurdles, technological barriers, and public perception, the potential benefits of blockchain in voting are significant. As jurisdictions explore innovative solutions to improve electoral processes, blockchain may play a pivotal role in shaping the future of voting.

Chapter 5

Blockchain for Intellectual Property and Copyright

Intellectual property (IP) is crucial for fostering creativity, innovation, and economic growth in our increasingly digital world. The protection of copyrights, trademarks, patents, and trade secrets enables creators and inventors to monetize their work and invest in new ideas. However, the traditional systems for managing and enforcing intellectual property rights are often inadequate, facing challenges such as piracy, counterfeiting, and a lack of transparency.

Blockchain technology offers a promising solution to these problems by providing a secure, decentralized, and transparent platform for managing intellectual property rights. By leveraging the unique features of blockchain, stakeholders can establish a more efficient, accountable, and trustworthy system for protecting and monetizing intellectual property.

In this chapter, we will explore how blockchain technology can transform the landscape of intellectual property and copyright management, focusing on its applications, benefits, challenges, and future potential.

Understanding Intellectual Property

Types of Intellectual Property

Intellectual property can be categorized into several key types, each serving a unique purpose and providing different forms of protection:

- **Copyright:** Copyright protects original works of authorship, including literary, musical, and artistic creations. It grants the creator exclusive rights to reproduce, distribute, and publicly display their work.

- **Trademark:** A trademark is a recognizable sign, logo, or expression that distinguishes products or services of one entity from those of others. Trademark protection prevents unauthorized use of marks that may confuse consumers.

- **Patent:** Patents grant inventors exclusive rights to their inventions for a specified period, typically 20 years. This protection encourages innovation by allowing inventors to profit from their inventions without fear of competition.

- **Trade Secret:** Trade secrets encompass confidential information that provides a competitive advantage, such as formulas, processes, or customer lists. Unlike other forms of IP, trade secrets are protected as long as they remain confidential.

The Importance of Intellectual Property

Intellectual property plays a vital role in driving innovation and creativity. By protecting the rights of creators and inventors, IP encourages investment in new ideas and products, leading to economic growth. Some key benefits of intellectual property include:

- **Encouraging Creativity:** IP protection incentivizes individuals and companies to create new works and inventions, knowing they can monetize their efforts.

- **Promoting Fair Competition:** IP rights help ensure that creators can compete fairly in the marketplace, preventing unauthorized copying and counterfeiting.

- **Facilitating Investment:** Investors are more likely to fund projects with strong IP protection, as it provides a clearer pathway to profitability.

- **Enhancing Brand Value:** Trademarks contribute to brand recognition and loyalty, adding value to businesses and their products.

The Challenges of Traditional IP Management

Piracy and Counterfeiting

The rise of the digital economy has made it easier for individuals to infringe on intellectual property rights. Piracy and counterfeiting pose significant threats to creators and businesses, resulting in lost revenue and diminished brand value. Traditional enforcement mechanisms can be slow and costly, leaving many creators vulnerable to infringement.

Lack of Transparency and Accountability

The traditional IP management system often lacks transparency, making it challenging for creators to track the use of their work and enforce their rights. The complexity of IP law, combined with jurisdictional differences, can create confusion and lead to disputes.

High Costs of Enforcement

Enforcing intellectual property rights can be prohibitively expensive, particularly for small businesses and individual creators. Legal fees, litigation costs, and the time required to pursue infringement cases can deter many from taking action against violators.

Difficulty in Licensing and Monetization

Licensing intellectual property can be a complex process, with various intermediaries involved. This complexity can lead to inefficiencies, delays, and a lack of trust among parties. Creators may struggle to find fair compensation for their work, leading to lost opportunities for monetization.

Applications of Blockchain in Intellectual Property

Blockchain technology has the potential to address many challenges associated with traditional intellectual property management. Some key applications include:

- **Provenance and Ownership Tracking:** Blockchain can provide a secure and transparent record of ownership and provenance for intellectual property. By recording each transaction on the blockchain, stakeholders can verify the authenticity of a work and its ownership history.

- **Digital Rights Management:** Blockchain can facilitate digital rights management (DRM) by enabling creators to control how their work is used and distributed. Smart contracts can automate licensing agreements, ensuring that creators receive fair compensation for the use of their work.

- **Copyright Registration:** Blockchain can streamline the copyright registration process by creating a tamper-proof record of original works. This can help establish authorship and provide evidence in cases of infringement.

- **Anti-Piracy Measures:** By providing a transparent record of ownership and licensing agreements, blockchain can deter piracy and counterfeiting. Stakeholders can easily track the use of their work and enforce their rights.

- **Decentralized Marketplaces:** Blockchain can enable the creation of decentralized marketplaces for buying and selling intellectual property. These platforms can facilitate peer-to-peer transactions, reducing the need for intermediaries and increasing transparency.

Case Studies: Blockchain in Action for Intellectual Property

Ascribe: Ownership Tracking for Digital Art

Ascribe is a blockchain-based platform that allows artists to register and track their digital art. By providing a secure record of ownership and provenance, Ascribe helps artists protect their work from infringement and unauthorized use.

Through Ascribe, artists can create digital certificates of authenticity for their art, which are recorded on the blockchain. This transparency allows collectors and buyers to verify the authenticity of the artwork and its ownership history.

Ujo Music: Revolutionizing Music Licensing

Ujo Music is a blockchain-based platform that aims to revolutionize the music industry by streamlining licensing and royalty payments. By enabling artists to register their music on the blockchain, Ujo Music provides a transparent record of ownership and usage rights.

Through smart contracts, Ujo Music automates royalty payments, ensuring that artists receive fair compensation for their work. The platform allows musicians to maintain control over their rights and directly engage with their audience.

Everledger: Securing the Wine Supply Chain

Everledger is a blockchain-based platform that provides transparency and traceability in the wine supply chain. By recording information about each bottle of wine on the blockchain, Everledger helps combat counterfeiting and ensures authenticity.

Wine producers can register their products on the Everledger platform, creating a secure record of ownership and provenance. This transparency not only protects the interests of producers but also enhances consumer confidence in the authenticity of the wine.

Myco: Protecting Sustainable Forestry

Myco is a blockchain-based platform that aims to protect sustainable forestry by providing a transparent record of timber ownership and sourcing. By registering timber on the blockchain, Myco helps ensure that only sustainably sourced wood enters the market.

Through Myco, stakeholders can track the supply chain of timber products, providing consumers with confidence in the sustainability of their purchases. This transparency helps combat illegal logging and promotes responsible forestry practices.

Benefits of Blockchain for Intellectual Property

Enhanced Security and Trust

Blockchain technology enhances the security and trustworthiness of intellectual property management. By providing a tamper-proof record of ownership and usage rights, stakeholders can confidently engage in transactions without fear of fraud.

Increased Efficiency and Cost Savings

Blockchain can streamline various processes associated with intellectual property management, reducing the need for intermediaries and lowering costs. Automating licensing agreements through smart contracts can significantly expedite the licensing process, benefiting both creators and consumers.

Greater Transparency and Accountability

The transparency of blockchain enables all stakeholders to access the same information regarding ownership and licensing agreements. This transparency fosters trust among participants and helps prevent disputes.

Empowering Creators and Innovators

Blockchain technology empowers creators and innovators by providing them with greater control over their work. By enabling direct engagement with consumers and facilitating fair compensation, blockchain can help ensure that creators are rewarded for their contributions.

Encouraging Collaboration and Innovation

The decentralized nature of blockchain fosters collaboration among stakeholders in the intellectual property ecosystem. By providing a secure platform for sharing ideas and resources, blockchain can encourage innovation and creativity.

Challenges and Considerations

Regulatory and Legal Frameworks

The legal and regulatory landscape for intellectual property is complex and varies by jurisdiction. As blockchain technology continues to evolve, policymakers must establish clear guidelines for the use of blockchain in IP management to ensure compliance with existing laws.

Technical Limitations

While blockchain technology offers significant advantages, it is not without limitations. Issues such as scalability, interoperability, and the energy consumption associated with some blockchain networks must be addressed to ensure widespread adoption.

Public Perception and Education

Public perception of blockchain technology can be a barrier to adoption. Educating stakeholders about the benefits and capabilities of blockchain in IP management is essential for overcoming skepticism and fostering acceptance.

Digital Divide and Accessibility Issues

While blockchain has the potential to enhance access to intellectual property rights, the digital divide remains a challenge. Ensuring that all stakeholders have access to the necessary technology and internet connectivity is crucial for the success of blockchain-based IP management solutions.

Future Directions for Blockchain in Intellectual Property

Collaborative Platforms for IP Management

As blockchain technology continues to mature, we may see the emergence of collaborative platforms that enable stakeholders to manage their intellectual property rights collectively. These platforms can facilitate communication, streamline processes, and enhance transparency.

Integration with Other Technologies

The integration of blockchain with other emerging technologies, such as artificial intelligence (AI) and the Internet of Things (IoT), has the potential to revolutionize intellectual property management. For example, AI can analyze usage patterns to optimize licensing agreements, while IoT devices can track the provenance of physical products.

Global Standardization

The development of global standards for blockchain-based IP management will be crucial for ensuring interoperability and facilitating cross-border transactions. Stakeholders must work together to establish best practices and guidelines that promote consistency and reliability.

Ongoing Research and Development

Continued research and development in blockchain technology will be essential for addressing existing challenges and unlocking its full potential for intellectual property management. Innovations in scalability, security, and usability can enhance the effectiveness of blockchain solutions.

Summary Thoughts

Blockchain technology has the potential to transform the landscape of intellectual property and copyright management. By providing a secure, transparent, and efficient platform for managing IP rights, blockchain can address many of the challenges associated with traditional systems.

As stakeholders explore innovative solutions to enhance intellectual property protection and monetization, blockchain may play a pivotal role in shaping the future of creativity and innovation. By empowering creators and fostering collaboration, blockchain technology can help ensure that the rights of intellectual property owners are respected and upheld in an increasingly digital world.

Chapter 6

Blockchain in Real Estate

The real estate industry is one of the largest and most influential sectors of the global economy. It encompasses a wide array of activities, including buying, selling, leasing, and managing properties. Despite its significance, the industry has long been plagued by inefficiencies, lack of transparency, and complex transaction processes. Traditional methods often involve numerous intermediaries, extensive paperwork, and a high risk of fraud.

Blockchain technology, with its decentralized and transparent nature, offers a promising solution to many of these challenges. By enabling secure, tamper-proof transactions and streamlining processes, blockchain has the potential to revolutionize the real estate landscape. This chapter will explore how blockchain technology is transforming real estate, its applications, benefits, challenges, and future prospects.

The Real Estate Landscape

The real estate industry encompasses various sectors, including residential, commercial, industrial, and agricultural properties. Each sector has its own unique characteristics and challenges. Despite these differences, common issues exist across the industry:

- **Inefficient Transactions:** Traditional real estate transactions involve multiple intermediaries, such as brokers, agents, and title companies. This complexity can lead to delays, increased costs, and frustration for buyers and sellers.

- **Lack of Transparency:** Many real estate transactions lack transparency, making it difficult for stakeholders to trust the information being presented. This lack of transparency can result in disputes and dissatisfaction.

- **Fraud and Security Risks:** The real estate industry is susceptible to fraud, including title fraud, identity theft, and mortgage fraud. Traditional systems often struggle to verify the authenticity of documents and ownership.

- **High Costs:** The costs associated with real estate transactions, including fees for agents, appraisers, and legal services, can be significant. These costs can deter potential buyers and create barriers to entry.

How Blockchain Can Transform Real Estate

Property Title Management

One of the most significant applications of blockchain technology in real estate is in property title management. Traditionally, maintaining accurate and secure property records has been a complex and labor-intensive process, often leading to disputes and confusion.

- **Immutable Land Registries:** Blockchain can create immutable land registries that provide a tamper-proof record of property ownership. By recording each transaction on the blockchain, stakeholders can verify the authenticity of title claims and track ownership history.

- **Streamlined Title Searches:** Traditional title searches can be time-consuming and costly. Blockchain can simplify this process by providing a single, transparent source of truth for property records, reducing the time and resources required for title verification.

Smart Contracts for Real Estate Transactions

Smart contracts are self-executing contracts with the terms of the agreement directly written into code. In real estate, smart contracts can automate various processes, enhancing efficiency and reducing the need for intermediaries.

- **Automated Escrow Services:** Smart contracts can facilitate automated escrow services, ensuring that funds are only released when all terms of the agreement are met. This automation reduces the risk of disputes and increases trust among parties.

- **Conditional Payments:** Smart contracts can enable conditional payments based on specific milestones, such as the completion of inspections or the transfer of ownership. This feature provides a clear framework for transactions and enhances accountability.

Tokenization of Real Estate Assets

Tokenization involves creating digital tokens that represent ownership of a real estate asset. These tokens can be bought, sold, and traded on blockchain platforms, enabling fractional ownership and increasing liquidity.

- **Access to Investment Opportunities:** Tokenization allows investors to purchase fractional shares of real estate assets, making it easier for individuals to invest in properties that may have previously been out of reach.

- **Increased Liquidity:** By enabling the trading of tokenized assets, blockchain can increase liquidity in the real estate market. Investors can easily buy and sell their tokens, creating a more dynamic marketplace.

Enhanced Transparency and Trust

Blockchain's transparent nature promotes trust among stakeholders in the real estate industry. By providing a secure and accessible record of transactions, blockchain can reduce the potential for fraud and disputes.

- **Clear Ownership Records:** With blockchain, all property ownership records are accessible and verifiable, ensuring that buyers and sellers can trust the information being presented.

- **Audit Trails:** Blockchain provides an immutable audit trail of transactions, allowing stakeholders to trace the history of a property and verify its legitimacy.

Case Studies: Blockchain in Action in Real Estate

Propy: A Platform for Global Real Estate Transactions

Propy is a blockchain-based platform that aims to simplify real estate transactions on a global scale. By providing a secure and transparent marketplace, Propy enables buyers, sellers, and agents to connect and conduct transactions with confidence.

- **International Transactions:** Propy allows users to conduct cross-border transactions with ease, eliminating the complexities associated with currency exchange and legal requirements in different jurisdictions.

- **Smart Contracts:** Propy utilizes smart contracts to automate various aspects of the transaction process, including escrow services and title transfers.

RealT: Tokenizing Real Estate Investments

RealT is a platform that enables the tokenization of real estate properties, allowing investors to purchase fractional ownership of income-generating assets. Through RealT, investors can buy tokens representing their share of a property, receiving rental income proportional to their ownership.

- **Fractional Ownership:** RealT democratizes real estate investment by enabling individuals to invest in properties with lower capital requirements.

- **Transparent Revenue Distribution:** The platform utilizes blockchain to automate rental income distribution to token holders, ensuring transparency and accountability.

Property Vault: Streamlining Real Estate Transactions

Property Vault is a blockchain-based platform designed to streamline the buying, selling, and leasing of properties. By leveraging blockchain technology, Property Vault provides a secure and efficient solution for real estate transactions.

- **Digital Title Management:** Property Vault offers a digital title management system that allows property owners to securely manage their titles on the blockchain.

- **Smart Contracts for Leasing:** The platform enables landlords and tenants to enter into smart contracts for leasing agreements, automating payment processes and reducing the risk of disputes.

Benefits of Blockchain in Real Estate

Increased Efficiency

By automating various processes and reducing the need for intermediaries, blockchain technology can significantly enhance efficiency in real estate transactions. This increased efficiency can lead to faster transactions and reduced costs for all parties involved.

Improved Security

Blockchain's immutable nature provides enhanced security for real estate transactions. With tamper-proof records and transparent ownership histories, stakeholders can trust that the information being presented is accurate and legitimate.

Greater Transparency

The transparent nature of blockchain fosters trust among stakeholders in the real estate industry. By providing a clear record of ownership and transaction history, blockchain can reduce the potential for disputes and misunderstandings.

Enhanced Accessibility

Blockchain technology has the potential to democratize access to real estate investment opportunities. By enabling fractional ownership and tokenization, individuals can invest in properties with lower capital requirements.

Reduced Fraud

Blockchain's secure and transparent nature helps mitigate the risk of fraud in real estate transactions. With verifiable ownership records and immutable transaction histories, stakeholders can have greater confidence in the legitimacy of property claims.

Challenges and Considerations

Regulatory and Legal Frameworks

The regulatory landscape for blockchain technology in real estate is still evolving. Policymakers must establish clear guidelines for the use of blockchain in real estate transactions to ensure compliance with existing laws.

Integration with Legacy Systems

Integrating blockchain technology with existing real estate systems and processes can be challenging. Stakeholders must work to ensure that new blockchain solutions are compatible with traditional practices and technologies.

Public Perception and Education

Public perception of blockchain technology can be a barrier to adoption. Educating stakeholders about the benefits and capabilities of blockchain in real estate is essential for overcoming skepticism and fostering acceptance.

Technical Limitations

While blockchain offers significant advantages, it is not without limitations. Issues such as scalability, interoperability, and the energy consumption associated with some blockchain networks must be addressed to ensure widespread adoption.

Future Directions for Blockchain in Real Estate

Integration with Internet of Things (IoT)

The integration of blockchain with IoT technology has the potential to revolutionize real estate management. By connecting smart devices to the blockchain, stakeholders can gain real-time insights into property performance, maintenance needs, and energy usage.

Enhanced Data Analytics

Blockchain technology can facilitate the collection and analysis of real estate data, providing stakeholders with valuable insights into market trends and consumer preferences. This data-driven approach can enhance decision-making and improve overall efficiency.

Global Standardization

The development of global standards for blockchain-based real estate transactions will be crucial for ensuring interoperability and facilitating cross-border transactions. Stakeholders must work together to establish best practices and guidelines that promote consistency and reliability.

Ongoing Research and Development

Continued research and development in blockchain technology will be essential for addressing existing challenges and unlocking its full potential in the real estate sector. Innovations in scalability, security, and usability can enhance the effectiveness of blockchain solutions.

Summary Thoughts

Blockchain technology has the potential to transform the real estate industry by enhancing efficiency, security, and transparency. As stakeholders explore innovative solutions to address existing challenges, blockchain may play a pivotal role in shaping the future of real estate transactions.

By empowering buyers, sellers, and investors with secure and transparent tools, blockchain technology can help create a more accessible and trustworthy real estate market. As the industry continues to evolve, embracing blockchain will be essential for unlocking new opportunities and driving growth in the real estate sector.

Chapter 7

Blockchain in Finance Beyond Cryptocurrencies

The financial landscape has undergone dramatic changes in recent years, fueled by advancements in technology and a growing demand for transparency, security, and efficiency. While cryptocurrencies like Bitcoin and Ethereum have garnered significant attention, the underlying technology—blockchain—offers a wealth of applications that extend far beyond the realm of digital currencies. Blockchain technology is poised to transform various aspects of finance, including payments, lending, asset management, and regulatory compliance.

This chapter explores the multifaceted applications of blockchain in finance beyond cryptocurrencies, highlighting its potential to enhance efficiency, security, and transparency in financial services. We will delve into specific use cases, benefits, challenges, and future trends shaping the landscape of finance in the blockchain era.

The Traditional Financial Landscape

The traditional financial system is characterized by various intermediaries, including banks, payment processors, and regulatory bodies. While these institutions play crucial roles in facilitating transactions and managing risk, they also introduce inefficiencies and costs. Common challenges in the traditional financial landscape include:

- **High Transaction Costs:** Intermediaries often charge fees for their services, resulting in higher costs for consumers and businesses.

- **Slow Transaction Times:** Cross-border transactions can take days to process due to the involvement of multiple institutions and regulatory compliance requirements.

- **Limited Access to Financial Services:** Many individuals and businesses, particularly in developing regions, lack access to basic financial services, hindering economic growth and inclusion.

- **Data Security Concerns:** The centralization of sensitive financial data makes traditional systems vulnerable to cyberattacks and data breaches.

Key Applications of Blockchain in Finance

Cross-Border Payments

Cross-border payments have traditionally been slow, costly, and fraught with complexities due to the involvement of multiple banks and payment providers. Blockchain technology can revolutionize this process by enabling faster and cheaper transactions.

- **Real-Time Settlements:** Blockchain allows for near-instantaneous settlements, reducing the time required for cross-border transactions from days to minutes.

- **Lower Fees:** By eliminating intermediaries, blockchain can significantly reduce transaction fees, making cross-border payments more accessible for individuals and businesses.

- **Increased Transparency:** Blockchain's transparent nature provides a clear audit trail of transactions, enhancing accountability and trust among participants.

Case Study: Ripple

Ripple is a blockchain-based payment protocol that facilitates real-time cross-border payments. Ripple's network allows financial institutions to settle transactions in real time, significantly reducing costs and improving efficiency. Ripple's digital asset, XRP, is used as a bridge currency, enabling seamless exchanges between different fiat currencies.

Trade Finance

Trade finance involves the financing of goods and services in international trade, often requiring multiple documents and parties to facilitate transactions. Blockchain can streamline trade finance processes by enhancing transparency and reducing fraud.

- **Document Digitization:** Blockchain can digitize trade documents, such as bills of lading and letters of credit, creating a secure and immutable record of transactions.

- **Smart Contracts for Automation:** Smart contracts can automate various aspects of trade finance, such as payment release upon delivery of goods, reducing the need for manual intervention.

- **Real-Time Tracking:** Blockchain enables real-time tracking of goods throughout the supply chain, enhancing visibility and reducing the risk of disputes.

Case Study: IBM TradeLens

IBM TradeLens is a blockchain-based platform designed to enhance transparency and efficiency in global trade. By connecting multiple stakeholders, including shipping companies, customs authorities, and importers, TradeLens enables real-time tracking of shipments and digitizes trade documents, streamlining the trade finance process.

Lending and Credit

Blockchain technology has the potential to disrupt traditional lending practices by providing new methods for credit assessment and loan origination.

- **Decentralized Lending Platforms:** Blockchain enables the creation of decentralized lending platforms that connect borrowers and lenders directly, eliminating the need for intermediaries.

- **Alternative Credit Scoring:** By leveraging blockchain data, lenders can access alternative credit scoring models that consider a broader range of data points, enhancing access to credit for underserved populations.
- **Smart Contracts for Loans:** Smart contracts can automate loan agreements, ensuring that funds are disbursed and repayments are managed transparently and efficiently.

Case Study: Aave

Aave is a decentralized lending platform that allows users to lend and borrow cryptocurrencies without intermediaries. Users can deposit assets to earn interest or take out loans by providing collateral. Aave utilizes smart contracts to automate the lending process, enhancing efficiency and reducing the risk of defaults.

Asset Management

Blockchain technology can enhance asset management by providing a secure and transparent platform for managing investments.

- **Tokenization of Assets:** Blockchain enables the tokenization of physical and digital assets, allowing for fractional ownership and increased liquidity in asset markets.

- **Transparent Reporting:** Blockchain's immutable ledger provides a transparent record of asset transactions, enhancing accountability and trust among investors.

- **Real-Time Portfolio Tracking:** Blockchain can facilitate real-time tracking of asset performance, providing investors with timely information for decision-making.

Case Study: CurioInvest

CurioInvest is a blockchain-based platform that allows investors to buy fractional ownership of luxury cars and collectibles. By tokenizing these assets, CurioInvest enhances liquidity and accessibility, enabling investors to diversify their portfolios and participate in alternative investment opportunities.

Regulatory Compliance and Reporting

Compliance with regulatory requirements is a significant burden for financial institutions. Blockchain technology can streamline compliance processes by providing secure and transparent records.

- **Automated Compliance Reporting:** Smart contracts can automate compliance reporting, ensuring that transactions adhere to regulatory requirements without manual intervention.

- **Real-Time Auditing:** Blockchain's transparent nature allows for real-time auditing of transactions, enhancing accountability and reducing the risk of fraud.

- **Secure Data Sharing:** Blockchain enables secure data sharing between financial institutions and regulators, facilitating compliance while protecting sensitive information.

Case Study: ComplyAdvantage

ComplyAdvantage is a blockchain-based platform that leverages machine learning and blockchain technology to enhance compliance processes. By providing real-time insights into regulatory risks and automating compliance reporting, ComplyAdvantage helps financial institutions navigate complex regulatory environments.

Benefits of Blockchain in Finance

Increased Efficiency

Blockchain technology can significantly enhance the efficiency of financial processes by automating manual tasks, reducing the need for intermediaries, and enabling real-time transactions. This increased efficiency can lead to cost savings and faster processing times.

Enhanced Security

Blockchain's decentralized and immutable nature enhances the security of financial transactions. By reducing the risk of fraud and data breaches, blockchain technology provides a secure platform for conducting financial activities.

Greater Transparency

The transparent nature of blockchain promotes trust among stakeholders in the financial ecosystem. By providing a clear audit trail of transactions, blockchain enhances accountability and reduces the potential for disputes.

Improved Access to Financial Services

Blockchain technology has the potential to democratize access to financial services by providing new avenues for lending, investment, and payments. By enabling decentralized platforms and alternative credit scoring methods, blockchain can empower underserved populations and foster financial inclusion.

Cost Savings

By eliminating intermediaries and streamlining processes, blockchain technology can significantly reduce transaction costs for consumers and businesses. This cost savings can make financial services more accessible and affordable.

Challenges and Considerations

Regulatory and Legal Frameworks

The regulatory landscape for blockchain technology in finance is still evolving. Policymakers must establish clear guidelines for the use of blockchain in financial services to ensure compliance with existing laws and protect consumers.

Integration with Legacy Systems

Integrating blockchain technology with existing financial systems can be challenging. Financial institutions must navigate compatibility issues and ensure that new blockchain solutions align with traditional practices.

Public Perception and Education

Public perception of blockchain technology can be a barrier to adoption. Educating stakeholders about the benefits and capabilities of blockchain in finance is essential for overcoming skepticism and fostering acceptance.

Technical Limitations

While blockchain offers significant advantages, it is not without limitations. Issues such as scalability, interoperability, and energy consumption associated with certain blockchain networks must be addressed to ensure widespread adoption.

Future Directions for Blockchain in Finance

Integration with Artificial Intelligence (AI)

The integration of blockchain with artificial intelligence (AI) has the potential to revolutionize financial services. AI can enhance data analysis and decision-making processes, while blockchain provides a secure and transparent platform for managing data.

Enhanced Data Analytics

Blockchain technology can facilitate the collection and analysis of financial data, providing stakeholders with valuable insights into market trends and consumer preferences. This data-driven approach can enhance decision-making and improve overall efficiency.

Global Standardization

The development of global standards for blockchain-based financial services will be crucial for ensuring interoperability and facilitating cross-border transactions. Stakeholders must work together to establish best practices and guidelines that promote consistency and reliability.

Ongoing Research and Development

Continued research and development in blockchain technology will be essential for addressing existing challenges and unlocking its full potential in the financial sector. Innovations in scalability, security, and usability can enhance the effectiveness of blockchain solutions.

Summary Thoughts

Blockchain technology is poised to transform the financial landscape by enhancing efficiency, security, and transparency. As financial institutions and stakeholders explore innovative solutions to address existing challenges, blockchain will play a pivotal role in shaping the future of finance beyond cryptocurrencies.

By empowering individuals and businesses with secure and accessible financial tools, blockchain technology has the potential to create a more inclusive and efficient financial ecosystem. As the industry continues to evolve, embracing blockchain will be essential for unlocking new opportunities and driving growth in the financial sector.

Chapter 8

Blockchain for Energy Markets

The global energy landscape is undergoing a transformative shift as the demand for sustainable and efficient energy sources continues to rise. With the advent of renewable energy technologies, decentralized energy generation, and the growing emphasis on energy efficiency, traditional energy markets are being challenged to adapt. In this context, blockchain technology emerges as a powerful tool that can enhance transparency, security, and efficiency in energy markets.

This chapter explores the multifaceted applications of blockchain in energy markets, detailing its potential to revolutionize energy trading, enhance grid management, facilitate peer-to-peer (P2P) energy trading, and promote sustainability. We will delve into specific use cases, benefits, challenges, and future trends shaping the energy sector in the blockchain era.

The Traditional Energy Market Landscape

The traditional energy market is characterized by centralized production and distribution systems, where a few large entities control the generation and supply of energy. This model has several drawbacks, including:

- **Inefficiencies:** Centralized systems can lead to inefficiencies in energy distribution and management, resulting in higher costs for consumers.

- **Limited Transparency:** Consumers often lack visibility into the sources of their energy, making it difficult to assess sustainability and environmental impact.

- **Regulatory Challenges:** The complex regulatory environment surrounding energy markets can create barriers to entry for new players and hinder innovation.

- **Vulnerability to Disruptions:** Centralized energy systems are vulnerable to disruptions, such as natural disasters or cyberattacks, which can lead to significant service interruptions.

Key Applications of Blockchain in Energy Markets

Peer-to-Peer (P2P) Energy Trading

Blockchain technology enables P2P energy trading, allowing consumers to buy and sell excess energy directly with one another. This decentralized approach promotes energy efficiency and sustainability.

- **Decentralized Marketplaces:** Blockchain can facilitate the creation of decentralized marketplaces where consumers can trade renewable energy generated from solar panels or wind turbines.

- **Smart Contracts for Automation:** Smart contracts can automate the trading process, ensuring that transactions are executed transparently and securely based on predefined conditions.

- **Increased Access to Renewable Energy:** P2P energy trading empowers consumers to engage in the renewable energy market, increasing access to clean energy sources and reducing reliance on fossil fuels.

Case Study: Power Ledger

Power Ledger is a blockchain-based platform that enables P2P energy trading. By connecting energy producers and consumers, Power Ledger allows users to trade excess solar energy directly, enhancing efficiency and promoting sustainability. The platform uses smart contracts to automate transactions, ensuring that trades are executed fairly and transparently.

Enhanced Grid Management

Blockchain technology can enhance grid management by improving data sharing, monitoring, and coordination among various stakeholders.

- **Real-Time Data Sharing:** Blockchain allows for real-time sharing of data related to energy production, consumption, and grid performance. This information can help grid operators make informed decisions and optimize resource allocation.

- **Decentralized Energy Storage:** Blockchain can facilitate decentralized energy storage solutions, allowing consumers to store excess energy generated from renewable sources and share it with the grid when needed.

- **Demand Response Programs:** Blockchain enables the implementation of demand response programs, where consumers can adjust their energy consumption based on grid conditions, promoting stability and efficiency.

Case Study: LO3 Energy

LO3 Energy is a blockchain-based platform that enhances grid management through real-time data sharing and decentralized energy trading. The company's Brooklyn Microgrid project allows local energy producers and consumers to trade energy within their community, improving grid resilience and promoting renewable energy adoption.

Renewable Energy Certificates (RECs) Tracking

Blockchain technology can streamline the tracking and verification of renewable energy certificates (RECs), ensuring transparency and accountability in the renewable energy market.

- **Immutable Records:** Blockchain provides an immutable record of REC transactions, reducing the risk of fraud and ensuring that renewable energy claims are verifiable.

- **Automated Verification:** Smart contracts can automate the verification process for RECs, ensuring that only eligible renewable energy sources receive certification.

- **Market Transparency:** Blockchain enhances transparency in the REC market, allowing consumers and businesses to track the sources of their energy and verify their sustainability claims.

Case Study: Energy Web Foundation

Energy Web Foundation (EWF) is a nonprofit organization that leverages blockchain technology to enhance the renewable energy market. EWF's platform enables the tracking and verification of RECs, providing stakeholders with a transparent and secure way to manage renewable energy transactions.

Decentralized Energy Management Systems

Blockchain technology can facilitate the development of decentralized energy management systems that empower consumers and businesses to optimize their energy consumption.

- **Consumer Empowerment:** Decentralized energy management systems allow consumers to monitor their energy usage in real-time, enabling them to make informed decisions about consumption and savings.

- **Incentives for Energy Efficiency:** Blockchain can enable incentive programs that reward consumers for reducing their energy consumption during peak demand periods, promoting sustainability and reducing strain on the grid.

- **Collaboration Among Stakeholders:** Decentralized energy management systems promote collaboration among stakeholders, including consumers, utilities, and regulators, to optimize energy usage and enhance grid stability.

Case Study: Grid+

Grid+ is a blockchain-based energy management platform that empowers consumers to take control of their energy usage. By providing real-time data on consumption and pricing, Grid+ enables consumers to optimize their energy use and save on costs. The platform also incentivizes users to participate in energy efficiency programs.

Carbon Trading and Offsetting

Blockchain technology can facilitate carbon trading and offsetting initiatives, promoting sustainability and reducing greenhouse gas emissions.

- **Transparent Carbon Markets:** Blockchain provides a transparent and secure platform for carbon trading, allowing stakeholders to buy and sell carbon credits with confidence.

- **Automated Tracking:** Smart contracts can automate the tracking of carbon credits, ensuring that transactions are executed accurately and efficiently.

- **Incentives for Emission Reductions:** Blockchain can enable incentive programs that reward businesses and individuals for reducing their carbon footprints, promoting sustainable practices.

Case Study: Verra

Verra is a nonprofit organization that oversees the Verified Carbon Standard (VCS), which certifies carbon offset projects. By leveraging blockchain technology, Verra aims to enhance transparency and accountability in carbon trading, providing stakeholders with a secure and reliable platform for managing carbon credits.

Benefits of Blockchain in Energy Markets

Increased Transparency

Blockchain technology enhances transparency in energy markets by providing an immutable record of transactions. This transparency promotes trust among stakeholders and reduces the potential for fraud and disputes.

Enhanced Efficiency

By automating processes and reducing the need for intermediaries, blockchain technology can significantly enhance the efficiency of energy transactions. This increased efficiency can lead to cost savings for consumers and businesses.

Improved Security

Blockchain's decentralized and immutable nature enhances the security of energy transactions. By reducing the risk of fraud and cyberattacks, blockchain provides a secure platform for conducting energy-related activities.

Greater Access to Renewable Energy

Blockchain technology promotes greater access to renewable energy by enabling P2P trading and decentralized energy management systems. This democratization of energy access empowers consumers and businesses to participate in the renewable energy market.

Sustainability and Environmental Impact

By facilitating carbon trading and promoting renewable energy adoption, blockchain technology contributes to sustainability and environmental stewardship. These initiatives can help mitigate climate change and promote a greener future.

Challenges and Considerations

Regulatory Frameworks

The regulatory landscape for blockchain technology in energy markets is still evolving. Policymakers must establish clear guidelines for the use of blockchain in energy transactions to ensure compliance with existing laws and protect consumers.

Integration with Existing Systems

Integrating blockchain technology with existing energy systems can be challenging. Energy providers must navigate compatibility issues and ensure that new blockchain solutions align with traditional practices.

Public Perception and Education

Public perception of blockchain technology can be a barrier to adoption. Educating stakeholders about the benefits and capabilities of blockchain in energy markets is essential for overcoming skepticism and fostering acceptance.

Technical Limitations

While blockchain offers significant advantages, it is not without limitations. Issues such as scalability, interoperability, and energy consumption associated with certain blockchain networks must be addressed to ensure widespread adoption.

Future Directions for Blockchain in Energy Markets

Integration with Internet of Things (IoT)

The integration of blockchain with IoT technologies has the potential to revolutionize energy management. IoT devices can provide real-time data on energy consumption and production, while blockchain can facilitate secure and transparent transactions based on this data.

Enhanced Data Analytics

Blockchain technology can facilitate the collection and analysis of energy data, providing stakeholders with valuable insights into consumption patterns and market trends. This data-driven approach can enhance decision-making and improve overall efficiency.

Global Collaboration

Global collaboration among stakeholders will be crucial for advancing blockchain technology in energy markets. Industry players, regulators, and researchers must work together to establish best practices and guidelines that promote interoperability and reliability.

Ongoing Research and Development

Continued research and development in blockchain technology will be essential for addressing existing challenges and unlocking its full potential in energy markets. Investing in innovative solutions and exploring new applications will drive growth and transformation in the sector.

Summary Thoughts

Blockchain technology holds immense potential for transforming energy markets by enhancing transparency, efficiency, and sustainability. By enabling P2P trading, improving grid management, streamlining REC tracking, and facilitating carbon trading, blockchain can empower stakeholders to create a more sustainable and efficient energy ecosystem.

As the energy landscape continues to evolve, embracing blockchain technology will be essential for overcoming existing challenges and unlocking new opportunities. With ongoing research, collaboration, and education, the future of energy markets in the blockchain era looks promising, paving the way for a greener and more inclusive energy future.

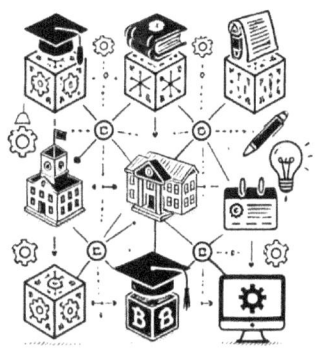

Chapter 9

Blockchain in Education

Education is a cornerstone of society, providing individuals with the knowledge and skills necessary to thrive in an increasingly complex world. However, traditional education systems face numerous challenges, including administrative inefficiencies, credential fraud, lack of transparency, and difficulty in tracking student progress. As technology continues to advance, innovative solutions are emerging to address these challenges, and blockchain technology stands out as a particularly promising tool.

Blockchain has the potential to revolutionize the education sector by enhancing the transparency, security, and efficiency of educational processes. This chapter explores the applications of blockchain in education, discussing its potential benefits, challenges, and future directions. We will delve into various use cases, including credential verification, student data management, learning analytics, and micro-credentialing.

Challenges in Traditional Education Systems

The traditional education system, while foundational, faces several significant challenges:

- **Credential Fraud:** The prevalence of fake degrees and certificates undermines the credibility of educational institutions and complicates the hiring process for employers.

- **Administrative Inefficiencies:** Managing student records, transcripts, and credentials often involves cumbersome paperwork and manual processes, leading to delays and errors.

- **Limited Student Control Over Data:** Students often lack control over their educational data, making it difficult for them to share their achievements and credentials with potential employers.

- **Lack of Transparency:** Educational institutions may not always provide clear and transparent information about their programs, policies, and accreditation status.

- **Difficulty in Tracking Learning Outcomes:** Traditional systems may struggle to track individual student progress effectively, hindering personalized learning experiences.

Key Applications of Blockchain in Education

Credential Verification

One of the most promising applications of blockchain technology in education is credential verification. By storing academic credentials on a blockchain, educational institutions can enhance the verification process and reduce the risk of fraud.

- **Immutable Records:** Academic credentials stored on a blockchain are immutable and can be easily verified by employers and other institutions. This reduces the chances of fraud and enhances the credibility of educational qualifications.

- **Instant Verification:** Blockchain enables instant verification of credentials, allowing employers to quickly assess a candidate's qualifications without the need for lengthy background checks.

- **Global Accessibility:** Storing credentials on a blockchain makes them accessible globally, allowing students to share their achievements with potential employers or educational institutions anywhere in the world.

Case Study: Learning Machine

Learning Machine is a company that leverages blockchain technology to provide secure and verifiable digital credentials. By partnering with educational institutions, Learning Machine enables the issuance of blockchain-based diplomas and certificates that can be easily verified by employers and other stakeholders.

Student Data Management

Blockchain can streamline student data management by providing a secure and transparent way to store and share student records.

- **Unified Student Profiles:** Blockchain allows for the creation of unified student profiles that aggregate academic achievements, extracurricular activities, and personal information in a single, secure location.

- **Student Control Over Data:** Students can have greater control over their educational data, deciding who can access their records and for what purposes.

- **Secure Data Sharing:** Blockchain provides a secure way for students to share their academic records with employers, educational institutions, or other stakeholders, eliminating the need for paper transcripts.

Case Study: ODEM

ODEM is a blockchain-based education marketplace that allows students to manage their educational records and credentials securely. Through ODEM, students can create and share their academic profiles with employers and educational institutions, enhancing transparency and control over their data.

Micro-Credentialing

Micro-credentialing refers to the practice of recognizing smaller, specialized achievements or skills. Blockchain can facilitate the issuance and verification of micro-credentials, promoting lifelong learning and skill development.

- **Stackable Credentials:** Blockchain enables the creation of stackable credentials, allowing students to build their qualifications incrementally by earning micro-credentials that can be combined into larger certifications.

- **Personalized Learning Pathways:** By offering micro-credentials, educational institutions can create personalized learning pathways that align with individual students' career goals and interests.

- **Employer Recognition:** Blockchain-based micro-credentials can enhance employability by providing employers with verifiable proof of specific skills and achievements.

Case Study: Purdue University

Purdue University has implemented a blockchain-based micro-credentialing system that allows students to earn and share digital badges for specific skills and achievements. These badges are stored on a secure blockchain and can be easily shared with employers and other institutions.

Learning Analytics

Blockchain technology can enhance learning analytics by providing a secure and transparent way to track and analyze student performance data.

- **Comprehensive Data Collection:** Blockchain allows for the collection of comprehensive data related to student performance, engagement, and learning outcomes, enabling educators to gain valuable insights into student progress.

- **Personalized Feedback:** Educators can leverage blockchain-based analytics to provide personalized feedback to students, helping them identify areas for improvement and tailor their learning experiences.

- **Improved Curriculum Design:** By analyzing data on student performance, educational institutions can make informed decisions about curriculum design and improvement, ensuring that programs meet the needs of students and employers.

Case Study: IBM and the University of Melbourne

IBM and the University of Melbourne collaborated to develop a blockchain-based learning analytics system. This system tracks student performance and engagement in real-time, providing educators with insights to enhance teaching and learning.

Enhanced Administrative Processes

Blockchain technology can streamline administrative processes within educational institutions, reducing inefficiencies and improving service delivery.

- **Automated Administrative Tasks:** Smart contracts can automate administrative tasks, such as enrollment, registration, and transcript issuance, reducing the burden on administrative staff.

- **Secure Funding and Financial Aid Management:** Blockchain can enhance the management of funding and financial aid by providing transparent records of transactions and ensuring that funds are allocated efficiently.

- **Accreditation Management:** Blockchain can facilitate the accreditation process by providing a secure and transparent way to track compliance with accreditation standards.

Case Study: The University of Nicosia

The University of Nicosia has implemented a blockchain-based platform to streamline administrative processes, including enrollment and transcript issuance. This initiative has reduced administrative burdens and improved efficiency for both staff and students.

Benefits of Blockchain in Education

Enhanced Security and Privacy

Blockchain technology enhances the security and privacy of educational records by providing a decentralized and immutable platform for storing sensitive information. This reduces the risk of data breaches and unauthorized access to student records.

Improved Trust and Transparency

By providing transparent and verifiable records, blockchain fosters trust among stakeholders, including students, employers, and educational institutions. This transparency enhances the credibility of educational qualifications and achievements.

Greater Control for Students

Blockchain empowers students by giving them greater control over their educational data. Students can manage their records, share them selectively, and track their progress in real-time.

Cost Savings and Efficiency

By automating administrative processes and reducing the need for intermediaries, blockchain technology can lead to significant cost savings for educational institutions. This efficiency allows institutions to allocate resources more effectively.

Lifelong Learning Opportunities

Blockchain enables the recognition of micro-credentials, promoting lifelong learning and skill development. This flexibility allows individuals to adapt to changing job markets and pursue continuous education.

Challenges and Considerations

Regulatory and Compliance Issues

The implementation of blockchain in education may face regulatory and compliance challenges. Policymakers must establish clear guidelines to govern the use of blockchain technology in educational settings.

Integration with Existing Systems

Integrating blockchain technology with existing educational systems can be complex. Educational institutions must navigate compatibility issues and ensure that new solutions align with traditional practices.

Public Awareness and Acceptance

Public awareness and acceptance of blockchain technology in education are crucial for successful implementation. Educators, students, and stakeholders must be educated about the benefits and capabilities of blockchain.

Technical Limitations

While blockchain offers significant advantages, it is not without limitations. Issues such as scalability, interoperability, and energy consumption associated with certain blockchain networks must be addressed to ensure widespread adoption.

Future Directions for Blockchain in Education

Integration with Artificial Intelligence (AI)

The integration of blockchain with AI technologies has the potential to enhance education further. AI can analyze data from blockchain networks to provide personalized learning experiences and improve student outcomes.

Global Collaboration and Standards

Global collaboration among educational institutions, regulators, and technology providers will be essential for advancing blockchain in education. Establishing common standards and best practices can promote interoperability and reliability.

Continued Research and Development

Ongoing research and development in blockchain technology will be crucial for unlocking its full potential in education. Investing in innovative solutions and exploring new applications will drive growth and transformation in the sector.

Enhanced Accessibility and Inclusivity

Blockchain technology can promote accessibility and inclusivity in education by providing secure and verifiable records for underserved populations. This can help bridge the gap for individuals who face barriers to traditional education systems.

Summary Thoughts

Blockchain technology has the potential to revolutionize the education sector by enhancing security, transparency, and efficiency. By facilitating credential verification, student data management, micro-credentialing, and learning analytics, blockchain empowers stakeholders to create a more equitable and effective educational ecosystem.

As the education system expands in the years to come, embracing blockchain technology will be essential for addressing existing challenges and unlocking new opportunities. With ongoing research, collaboration, and education, the future of education in the blockchain era looks promising, paving the way for more innovative educational experiences.

Chapter 10

Emerging Trends and Challenges for Blockchain

At this point in the book, you should better understand how blockchain can be used across a few industries. However, as blockchain continues to mature and find new applications, it also faces significant challenges that must be addressed to unlock its full potential. This chapter explores the emerging trends shaping the blockchain landscape and the challenges that could impede its widespread adoption and implementation.

Developing Trends in Blockchain Technology

Increased Adoption of Decentralized Finance (DeFi)

Decentralized finance, commonly referred to as DeFi, is a burgeoning sector within the blockchain ecosystem that aims to replicate traditional financial services using decentralized technologies. DeFi applications allow users to lend, borrow, trade, and earn interest on cryptocurrencies without the need for traditional intermediaries such as banks.

Key Drivers of Adoption

The increased adoption of DeFi is driven by several factors:

- **Access to Financial Services:** DeFi platforms provide access to financial services for individuals who are unbanked or underbanked, especially in developing regions. This democratization of finance allows anyone with an internet connection to participate in the global economy.

- **Lower Fees and Increased Efficiency:** By eliminating intermediaries, DeFi reduces transaction fees and enhances the speed of financial transactions. Users can engage in instant peer-to-peer transactions without the delays associated with traditional banking systems.

- **Innovation and Flexibility:** DeFi protocols offer a wide range of innovative financial products, including yield farming, liquidity mining, and synthetic assets, allowing users to maximize their returns and customize their financial strategies.

Challenges and Risks

Despite its rapid growth, the DeFi sector also faces challenges, including regulatory scrutiny, security vulnerabilities, and the potential for market manipulation. Ensuring consumer protection and regulatory compliance will be crucial for the long-term success of DeFi.

Integration with Central Bank Digital Currencies (CBDCs)

The Rise of CBDCs

Central banks around the world are exploring the concept of central bank digital currencies (CBDCs) as a response to the growing popularity of cryptocurrencies and the need for more efficient payment systems. CBDCs are digital representations of a country's fiat currency, issued and regulated by the central bank.

Benefits of CBDCs

The integration of CBDCs with blockchain technology could yield several benefits:

- **Enhanced Security and Trust:** By leveraging blockchain's inherent security features, CBDCs can provide a secure and trusted means of digital transactions.

- **Financial Inclusion:** CBDCs have the potential to promote financial inclusion by providing access to digital payment systems for individuals who lack access to traditional banking services.

- **Faster and Cheaper Transactions:** CBDCs can streamline payment processes, reducing transaction costs and settlement times.

Challenges Ahead

The implementation of CBDCs is not without challenges. Concerns about privacy, cybersecurity, and the potential impact on traditional banking systems must be carefully addressed. Additionally, regulatory frameworks will need to evolve to accommodate this new form of currency.

Interoperability Between Blockchain Networks

The Need for Interoperability

As the blockchain ecosystem continues to expand, the need for interoperability between different blockchain networks has become increasingly important. Interoperability refers to the ability of disparate blockchain networks to communicate and share data seamlessly.

Benefits of Interoperability

- **Enhanced Collaboration:** Interoperability enables collaboration between different blockchain projects, allowing for the development of more comprehensive solutions that leverage the strengths of multiple networks.

- **Increased Efficiency:** By facilitating the transfer of assets and data across various blockchains, interoperability can streamline processes and reduce friction in blockchain transactions.

- **Wider Adoption:** Interoperable blockchains can cater to a broader audience, attracting users and developers from different ecosystems.

Key Initiatives for Interoperability

Several projects and initiatives are working towards achieving interoperability, including:

- **Polkadot:** A multi-chain framework that allows different blockchains to communicate and share data securely.

- **Cosmos:** A decentralized network of independent blockchains that enables interoperability through the Inter-Blockchain Communication (IBC) protocol.

- **Chainlink:** A decentralized oracle network that facilitates communication between on-chain and off-chain data sources, promoting interoperability across different blockchain ecosystems.

Growth of Non-Fungible Tokens (NFTs)

Understanding NFTs

Non-fungible tokens (NFTs) have gained significant attention in recent years, particularly in the realms of art, gaming, and entertainment. Unlike cryptocurrencies such as Bitcoin or Ethereum, which are fungible and interchangeable, NFTs represent unique digital assets that cannot be exchanged on a one-to-one basis. NFTs exploded in popularity in the early 2020s, although the greater public didn't yet understand their value. So, while the NFT trend peaked quickly, the initial market crashed. There is a high probability of a resurgence in the NFT markets as the market expands and additional applications are created.

Market Expansion and Applications

The market for NFTs is expected to continue growing as new applications emerge, including:

- **Digital Art and Collectibles:** Artists can tokenize their work, allowing them to sell digital art directly to consumers while retaining ownership rights.

- **Gaming:** NFTs can represent in-game assets, enabling players to buy, sell, and trade unique items across different games.

- **Virtual Real Estate:** Platforms like Decentraland and Cryptovoxels allow users to buy and sell virtual land as NFTs, creating new opportunities for investment and creative expression.

Challenges and Criticisms

The NFT market is not without its challenges. Concerns about environmental sustainability, copyright issues, and market speculation have been raised. Addressing these challenges will be crucial for the long-term viability of the NFT space.

Enhanced Privacy Solutions

The Need for Privacy in Blockchain

As blockchain technology gains mainstream adoption, concerns about privacy and data security have become paramount. Many blockchain networks are public, meaning that transaction data is visible to anyone on the network, raising questions about user privacy.

Emerging Privacy Solutions

Innovations in privacy solutions are being developed to address these concerns:

- **Zero-Knowledge Proofs:** This cryptographic technique allows one party to prove to another that they know a value without revealing the value itself. This can enhance privacy in transactions while maintaining the integrity of the blockchain.

- **Privacy Coins:** Cryptocurrencies such as Monero and Zcash prioritize user privacy by implementing advanced cryptographic techniques that obscure transaction details.

- **Private Blockchains:** Some organizations are exploring the use of private or permissioned blockchains that limit access to transaction data, providing greater control over privacy.

The Balance Between Privacy and Transparency

Finding the right balance between privacy and transparency will be a key challenge for blockchain developers and regulators. Ensuring that privacy solutions comply with regulatory requirements while protecting user rights will be critical.

Adoption in Emerging Markets

Potential in Emerging Economies

Blockchain technology holds significant potential for driving economic development in emerging markets. By providing access to secure financial services, supply chain transparency, and efficient governance, blockchain can empower individuals and businesses in these regions.

Challenges to Overcome

While the potential benefits are substantial, challenges such as limited internet access, regulatory hurdles, and a lack of digital literacy must be addressed to facilitate blockchain adoption in emerging markets.

Increased Regulation and Compliance

Regulatory Landscape

As blockchain technology continues to evolve, regulatory scrutiny is expected to increase. Governments and regulatory bodies worldwide are working to establish frameworks that govern blockchain applications, particularly in sectors such as finance, healthcare, and data privacy.

The Role of Regulation

Regulation can play a crucial role in promoting the responsible use of blockchain technology:

- **Consumer Protection:** Regulations can safeguard consumers from fraud and abuse in the blockchain space, fostering trust in the technology.

- **Market Stability:** Regulatory frameworks can help prevent market manipulation and promote stability within the blockchain ecosystem.

- **Clarity for Businesses:** Clear regulations can provide businesses with guidance on compliance, facilitating innovation while minimizing legal risks.

Balancing Innovation and Regulation

Striking the right balance between fostering innovation and ensuring regulatory compliance will be a key challenge for policymakers. Engaging with industry stakeholders will be essential to create regulations that support growth while protecting consumers.

Focus on Sustainability

Environmental Concerns

The environmental impact of blockchain technology, particularly proof-of-work consensus mechanisms, has come under scrutiny. Critics argue that the energy consumption associated with mining activities contributes to climate change.

Sustainable Solutions

To address these concerns, the blockchain industry is exploring sustainable solutions:

- **Transition to Proof-of-Stake:** Many blockchain networks are transitioning from proof-of-work to proof-of-stake consensus mechanisms, significantly reducing energy consumption.

- **Carbon Offset Initiatives:** Some blockchain projects are implementing carbon offset initiatives to mitigate their environmental impact.

- **Sustainable Blockchain Projects:** A growing number of blockchain projects prioritize sustainability in their design and operations, focusing on renewable energy sources and eco-friendly practices.

The Role of Stakeholders

Stakeholders, including developers, investors, and regulators, will need to collaborate to promote sustainable practices within the blockchain ecosystem. Public awareness and support for sustainable blockchain initiatives will be essential for driving change.

Challenges Facing Blockchain Technology

The Scalability Dilemma

Scalability remains one of the most significant challenges facing blockchain technology. Many public blockchains struggle to process large volumes of transactions quickly and efficiently.

Potential Solutions

Several approaches are being explored to address scalability issues:

- **Layer 2 Solutions:** Technologies such as the Lightning Network for Bitcoin and Optimistic Rollups for Ethereum aim to process transactions off-chain while leveraging the security of the underlying blockchain.

- **Sharding:** Sharding involves dividing a blockchain network into smaller partitions, or shards, allowing for parallel processing of transactions and improved scalability.

- **Hybrid Solutions:** Combining public and private blockchains can provide the benefits of both while improving scalability.

The Importance of Scalability

Overcoming scalability challenges is crucial for achieving mass adoption of blockchain technology. Solutions that enable high transaction throughput will be essential for applications requiring real-time processing, such as financial services and supply chains.

Security Vulnerabilities

Cybersecurity Risks

As blockchain technology gains traction, concerns about security vulnerabilities become increasingly important. While blockchain is generally considered secure, it is not immune to attacks and exploits.

Types of Security Threats

- **Smart Contract Vulnerabilities:** Bugs and vulnerabilities in smart contracts can lead to significant financial losses, as seen in high-profile hacks.

- **51% Attacks:** In proof-of-work networks, if a single entity gains control of more than 50% of the network's mining power, it can manipulate transactions and double-spend.

- **Phishing and Social Engineering:** Users can fall victim to phishing attacks, leading to the theft of private keys and cryptocurrencies.

Enhancing Security Measures

Developers and organizations must prioritize security by implementing best practices, conducting audits, and educating users about potential threats. Collaboration within the blockchain community will also be essential for sharing knowledge and addressing vulnerabilities.

Regulatory Uncertainty

Evolving Regulatory Landscape

The regulatory landscape surrounding blockchain technology is continually evolving, leading to uncertainty for businesses and investors. Different jurisdictions have varying approaches to regulating blockchain and cryptocurrencies.

Implications of Regulatory Uncertainty

- **Investment Hesitancy:** Uncertainty about future regulations can deter investors from entering the blockchain space, limiting funding for innovative projects.

- **Compliance Challenges:** Businesses must navigate a complex regulatory environment, which can be resource-intensive and challenging to manage.
- **Stifling Innovation:** Overly stringent regulations may hinder innovation and prevent the development of new applications and use cases.

Advocating for Clear Regulations

Collaboration between industry stakeholders and regulators is essential for establishing clear and fair regulatory frameworks. Engaging in dialogue and advocacy can help shape regulations that foster innovation while ensuring consumer protection.

Public Perception and Understanding

Misconceptions about Blockchain

Public perception of blockchain technology is often shaped by misconceptions and a lack of understanding. Many people associate blockchain solely with cryptocurrencies, overlooking its broader applications and benefits.

Educating the Public

- **Awareness Campaigns:** Initiatives to educate the public about blockchain technology, its potential benefits, and real-world applications can help shift perceptions.

- **Case Studies and Success Stories:** Sharing success stories and case studies can demonstrate the practical applications of blockchain in various industries.

- **Collaboration with Educational Institutions:** Partnering with educational institutions to incorporate blockchain education into curricula can foster a more informed public.

Building Trust

Building public trust in blockchain technology is essential for driving adoption. Transparency, accountability, and effective communication will be key to overcoming skepticism and misconceptions.

Competition Among Blockchain Projects

Fragmented Ecosystem

The blockchain ecosystem is characterized by a multitude of projects and platforms, each vying for market share and adoption. This fragmentation can create confusion for users and businesses seeking to leverage blockchain technology.

Navigating Competition

- **Differentiation:** Projects must clearly articulate their unique value propositions and differentiate themselves in a crowded market.

- **Collaboration Over Competition:** Encouraging collaboration among blockchain projects can lead to shared resources, knowledge, and innovation, benefiting the entire ecosystem.
- **Focus on User Experience:** Prioritizing user experience and ease of use can attract users to blockchain applications, helping projects stand out in a competitive landscape.

The Future of Collaboration

As the blockchain ecosystem matures, collaboration may become increasingly important for driving innovation and adoption. Building partnerships and alliances can foster a more cohesive and interconnected blockchain landscape.

Summary Thoughts

The future of blockchain technology is both promising and challenging. As it continues to evolve, several key trends will shape its trajectory, including the rise of decentralized finance, the integration of central bank digital currencies, increased interoperability, and the growth of non-fungible tokens. However, the technology also faces significant challenges, including scalability issues, security vulnerabilities, regulatory uncertainty, and public perception.

To unlock the full potential of blockchain, stakeholders must work collaboratively to address these challenges and seize emerging opportunities. By fostering innovation, promoting education, and establishing clear regulatory frameworks, the blockchain ecosystem can continue to thrive and transform industries around the world.

Chapter 11

The Future of Blockchain Beyond Cryptocurrency

As we reflect on the transformative journey of blockchain technology, it becomes evident that its impact extends far beyond the realm of cryptocurrencies. While Bitcoin and Ethereum may have captured the public's attention, **the true power of blockchain lies in its potential to revolutionize numerous industries and redefine our approach to trust, transparency, and collaboration.** This conclusion aims to encapsulate the anticipated future of blockchain technology, its integration with emerging technologies, and the implications for businesses and individuals as we navigate this evolving landscape.

Enhanced Collaboration

Because of its decentralized nature, blockchain fosters a new paradigm of collaboration among businesses, individuals, and institutions.

Traditional systems often rely on centralized authorities, which can create bottlenecks and hinder cooperation. In contrast, blockchain enables stakeholders to work together on a shared, immutable ledger, promoting transparency and accountability.

As we saw in the chapter on supply chain management, blockchain allows all parties—from manufacturers to retailers—to access real-time information about the status and provenance of goods. This level of transparency not only builds trust among participants but also streamlines operations by reducing discrepancies and improving coordination.

Improved Efficiency

One of the most compelling advantages of blockchain is its ability to enhance operational efficiency. Businesses can significantly cut costs and time by automating processes through smart contracts and reducing the need for intermediaries. We discussed examples in the real estate industry, where blockchain facilitated property transactions by digitizing titles and automating the transfer process, eliminating lengthy paperwork and minimizing the risk of fraud.

Moreover, the integration of blockchain with emerging technologies such as artificial intelligence (AI) and the Internet of Things (IoT) will further augment efficiency. By combining these technologies, organizations can create interconnected systems that optimize decision-making and resource allocation. We reviewed how IoT devices can communicate data on energy consumption to a blockchain, allowing for real-time adjustments to energy distribution and usage patterns, ultimately leading to cost savings and sustainability.

Increased Security

With its cryptographic foundation, blockchain ensures that data is tamper-proof and secure, protecting sensitive information from unauthorized access. As industries grapple with data breaches and cyber threats, the inherent security features of blockchain provide a compelling alternative to traditional data storage and management systems.

The integration of blockchain with cybersecurity measures can enhance the protection of critical infrastructure, financial transactions, and personal data. We reviewed an example in the healthcare sector, where patient records stored on a blockchain are less vulnerable to breaches, ensuring patient privacy while facilitating secure sharing among healthcare providers.

The Convergence of Blockchain and Emerging Technologies

As we look to the future, the convergence of blockchain with emerging technologies such as AI, IoT, and big data analytics presents a wealth of new opportunities for innovation. This synergy holds the potential to create smarter systems and applications that can respond dynamically to real-time data.

Smart Contracts and IoT Integration

Combining blockchain with IoT allows for secure, automated processes that can operate without human intervention. For instance, in a smart home environment, IoT devices could communicate with a blockchain to manage energy consumption efficiently. Smart contracts can automate payments based on energy usage, ensuring fair compensation for energy producers while optimizing consumption for users.

This automation can extend to various sectors, including agriculture, where IoT sensors can monitor crop conditions and automatically trigger supply chain processes based on real-time data, enhancing food security and sustainability.

Big Data Analytics

The integration of blockchain with big data analytics will empower organizations to glean deeper insights from their data. By maintaining an immutable record of transactions and interactions, businesses can analyze patterns, identify trends, and make data-driven decisions. This analytical capability can lead to improved customer experiences, optimized operations, and more informed strategic planning.

As organizations leverage blockchain for data integrity, they will also enhance compliance with regulations and standards, particularly in industries such as finance and healthcare, where data accuracy and security are paramount.

Regulatory Frameworks Shaping Blockchain's Future

The evolution of regulatory frameworks will play a pivotal role in shaping the future of blockchain technology. As governments and institutions develop clear guidelines and standards, businesses will be more inclined to adopt blockchain solutions, knowing they operate within a compliant framework.

Navigating Regulatory Challenges

The regulatory landscape surrounding blockchain and cryptocurrencies is complex and varies significantly across jurisdictions. Businesses must navigate these challenges while ensuring compliance with evolving regulations. Engaging with policymakers and industry associations will be crucial for fostering an environment conducive to innovation.

As more jurisdictions establish regulatory clarity, businesses will be better equipped to explore blockchain applications confidently. A well-defined regulatory framework can also help to build public trust, encouraging wider adoption of blockchain solutions in everyday transactions and interactions.

Promoting Responsible Innovation

It is essential for stakeholders in the blockchain ecosystem to advocate for responsible innovation. By collaborating with regulators and participating in discussions about the future of blockchain, businesses can help shape policies that promote transparency, consumer protection, and ethical practices.

In this context, industry self-regulation and the establishment of best practices can enhance credibility and trust. By demonstrating a commitment to responsible innovation, blockchain projects can foster public acceptance and encourage widespread adoption.

Adopting Blockchain in Business and Daily Life

Individuals will increasingly encounter blockchain technology as it becomes integrated into various services and platforms. From securely managing personal data to engaging in decentralized financial systems, consumers will benefit from enhanced control over their digital lives. As public awareness grows, so too will the demand for transparency, security, and accountability in transactions and interactions.

Digital identity solutions based on blockchain will empower individuals to control their personal information, selectively sharing data with trusted parties while protecting their privacy. This shift towards self-sovereign identity represents a significant advancement in how we manage our digital presence.

Addressing Adoption Challenges

The path to widespread adoption of blockchain will not be without challenges. Issues such as scalability, security, and regulatory compliance must be addressed to unlock the full potential of this transformative technology. Collaboration among stakeholders, including developers, businesses, regulators, and the public, will be essential for overcoming these obstacles.

With continued innovation, dialogue, and collaboration, blockchain has the potential to reshape our world in profound and lasting ways. By fostering a spirit of cooperation, the blockchain community can work together to address challenges and seize opportunities for growth and development.

Summary Thoughts of this Book

The journey of blockchain technology is still in its early stages, and while the potential is immense, its successful adoption requires a concerted effort from stakeholders across various sectors. Businesses must be willing to invest in research and development to explore innovative applications of blockchain. They should also prioritize education and training for employees to foster a culture of understanding and adaptability.

Individuals will increasingly encounter blockchain technology as it becomes integrated into various services and platforms. From securely managing personal data to engaging in decentralized financial systems, consumers will benefit from enhanced control over their digital lives. As public awareness grows, so too will the demand for transparency, security, and accountability in transactions and interactions.

With continued innovation, collaboration, and dialogue, blockchain has the potential to reshape our world in profound and lasting ways. As we look ahead, it is evident that blockchain technology is not merely a trend but a fundamental shift in how we think about trust, transparency, and collaboration. Embracing this shift will enable businesses and individuals to navigate the complexities of the modern world with confidence and agility, paving the way for a more equitable and efficient future. In this ever-evolving landscape, the future of blockchain is bright, and its impact will resonate across industries and societies for generations to come.

www.ingramcontent.com/pod-product-compliance
Lightning Source LLC
Chambersburg PA
CBHW050311230526
45471CB00005B/2129